# The Naked Betrayal

A Guide to All Things Porn: How to Know
If Pornography Is Helping or Hurting You

*Original Edition*

SAGE WILCOX

The Naked Betrayal: A Guide to All Things Porn: How to Know If Pornography Is Helping or Hurting You

Copyright © 2019 Sage Wilcox

Find Your Way Publishing, Inc.
P.O. Box 667
Norway, ME 04268
www.findyourwaypublishing.com

*All rights reserved.* **No part of this book may be reproduced, stored in a retrieval system or transmitted in any form or by any means, electronic, mechanical, photocopying, recording, or otherwise, without the written permission of the publisher.**

First Edition, 2019

ISBN-13: 978-1-945290-29-9

ISBN-10: 1-945290-29-3

Printed in the United States of America.

# DEDICATION/ACKNOWLEDGEMENTS

This is dedicated to all the people who are working hard to better their lives and situations, day by day, in every way. Those who don't settle for mediocre will soar. Perseverance and discipline pay off. YOU deserve to make your dreams come true and reach your full potential, and this book is for you.

Deep, humble appreciation to the Divine Source, whom I aspire to grow closer to every day, in faith.

Thanks to all who made this book possible. And to those who share their stories and life experiences with me. We can learn so much from other people's life lessons.

And, most importantly, to the readers, thank you for taking the time to read this book. I hope it helps you find answers and inspires you in some way. If you find any of it beneficial please consider leaving a review. Reviews help more than you know. Thank you! Let's pour our favorite drink, find a comfortable spot, and get started, shall we? Our dreams and desires are waiting to be fulfilled.

# Other books by Sage Wilcox:

**Nonfiction:**

<u>Love Letters from Exes:</u> *Proof That Life Goes on After a Break Up and Love Is What You Make It*

<u>Get It Up:</u> *101 Ways to Raise Your Vibration, Reduce Stress, Depression, & Anxiety, Increase Joy, Peace, & Happiness and Attract Abundance Automatically!*

<u>The 2-Hour Vacation:</u> *Let Go and Relax, Reduce Stress & Anxiety, Gain Inner Peace, and Happiness*

<u>The Importance of Doing It:</u> *How to Utilize Discipline to Get Out of Bed, and Make Your Dreams Come True! A Guide to Taking Action to Create Successful Habits...*

<u>Less Is Best:</u> *Declutter, Organize, & Simplify to Reach Minimalism; Get More Time, Money, & Energy*

<u>You Had Me at Re: Hello:</u> *The Ultimate Guide to Online Dating, Including Tips and Testimonies*

<u>Neuroplasticity and the Default Mind:</u> *How to Shape Your Plastic Brain by Forming New Connections to Automatically Get Positive Results, Success and Prosperity*

<u>Adjust:</u> *How to Conquer and Accept Change and Adversity Swiftly; Stop Putting off the Love, Money, Peace, Success, and Happiness You Deserve Now*

<u>Born New:</u> *How to See the Familiar with New Eyes, Embrace the Magic of the Present Moment, Experience Satisfaction and Joy like Never Before*

<u>Level Up</u>: *How to Man Up and Excel When Society and Role Models Have Let You Down*

**Romance:**

    Until We Fall

    Under the Covers

    Photo Finish

    U-Turn

    Love in Troubled Waters

    Solitary Heart (With Heart Series #1)

    Awakened Heart (With Heart Series #2)

    Hopeful Heart (With Heart Series #3)

# Contents

True Intimacy and Fulfilling Relationships Explored .........1
  **Spicing it up in the bedroom** .................................1
Introduction .................................................................3
  **Effect on the Brain** .................................................6
  **Habits and Addiction** .............................................7
  **Hijacking Nature** ...................................................8
  **The Effects** ............................................................8
  **The Number One Sited Reason** ............................9
Chapter 1: The Route to Porn ....................................13
Chapter 2: The Brain On Porn ....................................17
Chapter 3: The Psychology of Pornography ..............21
  **Stage 1** ...................................................................21
  **Stage 2** ...................................................................22
  **Stage 3** ...................................................................23
  **Stage 4** ...................................................................24
  **Stage 5** ...................................................................25
  **The Physical Effects** .............................................26
Chapter 4: The World We Live In ...............................27
Chapter 5: What the Research Shows ........................31

- **Is Pornography Similar to Cheating? ....................... 32**
- **What the Brain Does............................................. 33**
- **Where Does Choice Come In? ............................... 34**
- **Does Pornography Use Lower Commitment?........... 38**
- **Pornography and Intimacy .................................... 39**
- **What Do Women Get Out of Pornography? ............. 40**
- **When It's Unhealthy ............................................. 42**

Chapter 6: Facts to Make You Think ................................. 47

Chapter 7: Is Addiction to Pornography a Real Thing? ..... 53

Chapter 8: Why Couples Turn to Pornography ................. 59

Chapter 9: Long Term Effects On Your Relationship ........ 63

Chapter 10: The Core of Marriage and Family ................. 67

Chapter 11: Creating Fulfilling and Rewarding Sexual Relationships ........................................................................ 69

Chapter 12: Testimonies ..................................................... 77

Conclusion ........................................................................... 93

- **Where to Next ...................................................... 94**

About Sage Wilcox ............................................................. 95

Please consider leaving a review, online, after reading this book. Reviews help more than you know, and don't have to be long; a few sentences will do. Thank you very much for your time and consideration. I am sincerely grateful.

Wishing many blessings to you and yours,

~Sage Wilcox

# True Intimacy and Fulfilling Relationships Explored

## Spicing it up in the bedroom

Have you been with your partner for a while? Do you ever find yourself falling into a routine? Want to spice up your relationship? Make it a little more exciting? Who doesn't, right? This is one of the biggest desires for couples who want their union to stay fresh and appealing. Thankfully, with the click of a few buttons, we can dim the lights and spice up our relationship and maybe even share a romantic evening together watching an X-rated movie. We laugh and joke as we watch and then make passionate love. No harm done, right?

Or, maybe you're single and looking for love. Thankfully, with the click of a few buttons, you can dim the lights and take care of yourself by watching a little porn while you wait for the love of your life to show up. No harm done, right?

I'm not here to tell you what to do, or what's right or wrong. (Some people don't believe pornography has any negative side effects.) I'm just here to give you the facts. Once you read through, you can decide for yourself. What I can tell you, though, is that it's not too late to have the relationship of your dreams.

This insightful book delves into some of the real issues facing couples today on the subject of sexual intimacy in relationships. With testimonies from real people and couples who had the very best intentions for their relationships, only to have unexpected, and often times, devastating results.

Did you know that viewing pornography causes impotence and erectile dysfunction, even in young healthy men? (Erectile dysfunction leads to low self-esteem, which leads to depression and on and on we go.)

Studies also show that relationships can be much more fulfilling, rewarding and better without pornography. You, or your partner, may be flirting with the idea of incorporating pornography in your relationship, or you may be actively using it, either way, you will find some interesting nuggets of information in this book. Join us as we explore the context around pornography in relationships; the pros and cons, pains and pitfalls, as well as some of the burning issues facing couples today who are longing to rekindle the fire in their relationship. We will also fill you in on proven tips and tools to revitalize your relationship in healthy and rewarding ways so you can maintain true satisfaction, passion, and happiness.

# Introduction

*"One man's pornography is another man's theology."* ~
Clive Barker

THE PRESSING ISSUE with pornography is not that it can be vile, sexist and objectify women. It's not just about subjecting the performers to subhuman conditions on and off camera, sometimes exposing them to potentially fatal conditions. It's not even that it is responsible for lost jobs and reduced productivity. And even though it is the single most potent reason behind the erosion of self-worth, the even bigger threat, the biggest in fact, is that consuming pornography is covertly addictive and can act as a wedge in an otherwise happy, real-life intimate relationship.

This subtle nature of the addiction results in two out of three men in the U.S. watching porn at least once a month. That number grows with time. One out of every five men above the age of 18, believes he is addicted to porn. 63% of men, and 30% of women below 30 watch porn several times a week. 1 out of 5 mobile Google searches is for pornographic material. And this is just the tip of the iceberg.

Smokers, alcoholics, and gamblers typically realize they have an addiction. People who watch porn, start off doing it for fun, then continue doing it without understanding why - they don't believe they are addicted. This is true across all ages. Research shows that the average age for getting started on porn is the tender age of 11. That number describes conventional media. With the prevalence of the internet, and an internet that is getting more personal (mobile devices), the average age to get started is now trending towards eight.

The insidious nature of porn is magnified because it is erroneously believed that porn is not a crime and that it is victimless. But when you do a little research you find that is not completely true.

Performers are subject to a life that is characterized by abuse, addiction, and psychological issues and stresses. 79% of performers are marijuana users, 38% use hallucinogens. Diseases are also rampant with 66% suffering from herpes, 28% have other forms of STD and 7% have HIV.

Consumers face a different sort of hazard. Spouses who indulge in pornography place their marriage in distress. There are increased incidences of infidelity, separation, and divorce; 56% of divorces stemmed from addictive behavior to pornography. There is a positive correlation across various studies showing that increased porn consumption leads to a reduced commitment to one's partner. This can result in infidelity, loss of interest in marriage and family, and extend to deviant sexual preferences. 71% of those addicted to porn exhibited severe dysfunctional symptoms in other parts of their lives as well. Read on for more info about that.

The true size of the porn industry is difficult to quantify. However, the demand can be approximated by the number of search engine queries. There are more than 60 million search engine requests daily; every second of the day has almost 30,000 computers logging on to a porn site; there are more than four million porn websites, and this number is escalating. 35% of all downloads are pornographic, and this number is also rising.

The irony, and the catastrophic consequence of all this, however, is that pornography can severely increase a person's fear of emotional intimacy. This, in turn, and in concert with other side effects of porn, damages, hinders and ultimately ruins the relationships we were hoping to enhance.

The two most important things in a person's life are found internally and externally. The internal is the person's mind. The external is the person's relationship with his soul mate and family. Pornography destroys both, slowly at first, then with increasing ferocity. Its effects are even more devastating owing to the easy-to-hide nature of the addiction, compounded by the fallacy that this type of sex is a natural human instinct. But make no mistake, pornography is not sex. Pornography is not natural. The calamity that follows in the wake of pornographic addiction is real. It crosses the space between two people and overflows to innocent children who are then marred for life.

That's the best-case scenario.

What about the worst case, you ask? Well, there doesn't seem to be a bottom to how far the destruction this addictive habit can lead to. While other addictions do not necessarily cross over to porn, porn can lead to alcohol and drug abuse. It leads to low self-esteem, depression, anxiety, and erectile dysfunction. It even has the potential to escalate to rape, incest, and murder.

None of these conduce a happy family life.

It is insufficient to claim pornography's ills without substantiating it beyond rhetoric. Aside from the statistics that encapsulate the correlation between pornography and a diminished life, we will need to show the medical effects of addiction, specifically pornography addiction, and how the brain responds from a chemical and psychological perspective.

## Effect on the Brain

The human mind is a robust construct, molded by what it is subjected to. We are designed, as a species, to endure and thrive. One of the mechanisms at our subconscious' disposal is the ability to desensitize from frequently occurring stimuli. When this same innate characteristic is applied to frequent arousing stimuli via pornography, the body begins to desensitize. This results in lower gratification with the progress of time. To maintain the same level of gratification requires the person to increase the nature of the stimuli and this usually results in deviant sexual practice, and addiction.

In a neurological study, groups were tested by conducting MRIs while they were shown advertisements for porn sites. The group that had little or no porn exposure showed no difference in the scan. The group that consumed porn daily had a physical response in the brain identical to that of an alcoholic while viewing an advertisement for alcohol.

Another neurological study found that grey matter mass in porn addicts showed significant degradation. In other words, the more a subject was addicted to porn, the smaller the volume of grey matter. This eventually has an effect on how the person handles other areas of their life including family, friends, and even being able to contribute positively towards his employment.

With reduced functional brain capacity, the everyday stresses of family life can become daunting. Make no mistake about it, this is a severe impairment and those afflicted with it deserve compassion just as any person suffering from any other affliction. The only difference is that in pornography consumption and addiction, the consumer has the choice to start down this path or not.

## Habits and Addiction

Porn addiction has a similar path across cultures. It typically starts with partial nudity or full frontal on easily available media. This stimulates curiosity and arousal.

In men, the part of the brain, the hypothalamus, that places importance on food and water is also triggered with the introduction of sexual material. The arousal is complicated because it is part of man's design to advance the species. But remember, porn is not sex and porn is not going to advance the species. Porn is like a mind hack. When the mind receives the stimuli, it releases pleasurable hormones upon gratification.

This causes the formation of a habit. Habits are formed when three factors come together. The stimuli, the act, and the reward. After a few times, the body naturally goes for the easiest path to the reward. Sex with a real-life partner is a little more complicated and the path to the reward is not as simple.

## Hijacking Nature

From species survival, porn has now hijacked the male instinct and created a habit. This puts us in striking distance of an addiction. The hormones released from the first arousal to the end of the session create such a strong bond to pornography, so much so, that a real person is then unable to replace "the high" that porn can easily offer.

## The Effects

How we frame the issue of pornography is important. It is not victimless. The consumer and spouse pay the toll, and in many cases so do the children. The health of one's mind is important in how much happiness we experience and how much happiness we create for those immediately around us.

Porn robs families of the presence of the father, or the mother, during times of gratification. In contrast with smoking, when the father needs to have a 'fix' he walks out of the room, finishes his cigarette, and comes back in. I'm not condoning smoking, just drawing a contrast. In porn addiction, however, when the urge triggers, the father needs to extract himself from his family for long periods and make excuses for his absence. That's just the beginning. With time, his taste grows more perverse and inadvertently he may seek out physical gratification that mimics his new definition of pleasure. A role that the spouse is either pressured into performing or not, thereby changing the dynamics of the relationship.

Or, the offending spouse seeks an outlet with more like-minded sexual partners outside the marriage. In some cases, the partner outside the marriage doesn't need to be like-minded, just submissive enough for the man to act out his perverted (porn induced) fantasies. Either way, the relationship with the spouse sours, and she is left not understanding what went wrong. 72% of women who go through divorce triggered by pornography, end up having symptoms similar to those suffering PTSD.

If you can look past all this, the one thing that's sure to grab your attention is the fact that while all this is going on with the adults, if children are involved, they are the ones witnessing the breakup of their sanctuary and being introduced to something that could rattle the rest of their lives as well.

Consuming porn doesn't make a person bad. Saying it does, is like saying a person who is addicted to cigarettes is bad. The altered state of the brain under MRIs is proof. A person who is under the influence of this addiction deserves medical attention and caring and compassionate intervention. It's something that, with awareness, could be curtailed before it starts. It's something that should be talked about openly because today's youth are a click away from some of the nastiest brands of pornography, and it will get worse with the advent of virtual reality.

## The Number One Sited Reason

There are many reasons why one might begin developing an interest in pornography and just as many varied roads that can lure one into making a habit of its use. Plain and simple, it produces instant gratification, but read on for a more detailed explanation.

One of the most often cited reasons for the usage of pornography is, of course, it's ability to replace the spark that was once felt in a relationship. Couples hope that it will help spice things up in the bedroom. It's a rare couple who can effortlessly keep intimate and passionate nights spontaneous and blood pumping for years to come. Eventually, boredom can set in as the "honeymoon phase" gradually turns into a well-oiled routine.

For others, however, the pornography habit may have been developed accidentally. Maybe you found temptation from an advertisement or a popup on your computer. Maybe you watched a sexy music video as a teen, and it enticed you to look at and search for more provocative videos. The World Wide Web hosts thousands of sites dedicated just to making a profit off the porn industry and they're constantly on the lookout and trying to hook in new consumers. As one of the biggest issues with pornography is easily the widespread influence and presence it holds, it can be, at times, hard to avoid. Eventually, a time may come when we will all run into a situation or setting where we will be confronted with it.

For some, during that spur of the moment decision where their sexual desires took over their rational thought process and first introduced them to the crippling ball and chain that pornography can develop into, they probably never considered the consequences of that simple decision. The usage of porn comes with a long line of questions that must be asked and answered. (It doesn't do us any good to ask questions if we aren't willing to answer them truthfully.) Many of these questions are hard personal ones that we may not want to directly confront. Confronting difficult subjects can be uncomfortable. Yet in this book, we will take a journey together to bring these topics to light as page by page we'll present information on pornography you might not have known before.

No matter what your reason for reading this book, whether it be from a lack of connectivity occurring in the bedroom or maybe you're noticing a negative change in your own sexuality or your partner's behavior. Maybe you just want to become better informed. We can't do better until we know better. And we can't help others until we know how. This book will certainly help you explore the ways pornography has affected your relationship with not just yourself, but also with those around you. Not only will you be informed of many things you may not know, on the topic of pornography, but you will also be presented with ways to help you reconnect with your sexuality and advice on how to mend the open wounds that can be left behind because of it.

If you're still uncertain if you should invest further time into this topic, then don't be doubtful any longer. There is longstanding and well-backed research that indicates the long-term effects of habitual pornography usage. And because it affects so many people, it's good to be made aware of it. Pornography can be fatal to one's relationships and to their own personal health and sexuality. This book is not meant to demean or lecture anyone about their choices. This book's purpose is merely to forewarn those unaware of pornography's side effects and to help those who have experienced a negative impact on their lives because of it. There is hope.

Of course, before one can even begin to reclaim what pornography has taken from them, they must first understand what they're up against. As was long ago said by Sun Tzu, "Knowledge of your enemy is paramount to success." So, I encourage and implore you to read on and arm yourself with the knowledge this book can impart upon you and take the first courageous step forward to facing these growing obstacles.

The main aim of this book is to present couples with up-to-date research and statistics on pornography. We also want to stimulate thought and help couples establish a well-rounded and solid opinion on their stance of pornography and how it should or shouldn't be considered in intimate relationships.

According to online statistics firms, an estimated forty million people use pornography on a habitual basis. This is of course excluding those isolated times of usage by many who don't find themselves needing the stimulation on a daily basis. Even still, that is quite a hefty number, forty million people. With such a widespread usage of pornography occurring and with all the negative repercussions, it creates it gives cause for concern. Thankfully there is something we can do about it.

***

## Chapter 1: The Route to Porn

> *"Erotica is simply high-class pornography; better produced, better conceived, better executed, better packaged, designed for a better class of consumer."* ~ Andrea Dworkin

THE GOOD NEWS, IF YOU could call it that, is that not everyone who watches porn will get addicted to it. Addiction is indeed a strong word to describe a habit that has become uncontrollable. However, porn appeals to the basest instinct of the male gender.

Most of the gender reference in this book is in the masculine. While it is for literary expediency to refer to one gender and mean both, referring to the males is also because more men are addicted to porn than are women. It is the biological makeup of the man's brain that predisposes him to seek out pornography, then becoming addicted to it. It is not a stereotype. Of course, this affects women as well, but it is a fact that 63% of men below 30 watch porn more than a few times in a week, among women, that number drops to 21%.

Even for those who have strong views against consuming pornography, contemporary culture in the entertainment and fashion industry serve as bait. There are two sides to the psychological coin.

One is curiosity. The repeated flashing of flesh creates a pleasurable response propelling the viewer to up the ante. Before long, friends introduce a certain website or pass a DVD. The rush of the first viewing is incomparable to anything else they've experienced until that point in their life. Curiosity is woven into the fabric of human nature. It's why we do so many of the things we do.

Two, we crave intimacy on a very deep level and there is nothing more intimate than someone comfortable enough to disrobe in your presence - even if that person is virtual. The short circuit here is that the disrobing is done by a performer who is paid (or forced) to do it and is probably stoned or drunk (the use drugs and alcohol to disassociate themselves from the act during filming.) And in reality, there is nothing intimate about the experience.

The female of the species is designed to behave provocatively while the male of the species is designed to take advantage of that - there is a trigger in the hypothalamus that prepares the males for sex, in street parlance, it's called getting turned on. It is a design in the two genders, and it serves a specific purpose - to propagate the species. It is through socialization and learning that members of both genders mitigate their base instincts.

There are a number of assumptions that pervade the collective psyche. These assumptions cross-ideological barriers and affect those who see porn in the broad 'bad' light and those who accept porn as a reality, neither good nor bad.

The first assumption is that porn is only bad for morals but does nothing to the health of the individual. The second assumption is that porn is an acceptable relief valve for those who need their sexual fantasies satisfied. Those with this perspective appreciate the existence of porn since they think it gets rapists and molesters off the street and into the basement across from their computer screens. Wrong. The reverse is true (we will cover this in the next chapter). Finally, they assume that the habit has no victim

Parents can unintentionally kick-start the problem by not adequately discussing the birds and the bees with their children. It's the beginning of the new millennium and yet 64% of parents still tell their kids about some fairytale as the story behind their question, "Mommy, where do I come from" or "Who made me?" As these children grow older, they start to get the feeling that there is something amiss and that their parents are keeping something from them. By around their 12th birthday, 40% of adolescents finally get their birds and the bees talk, and by this point, a friend or classmate has already clued them in. Since first impressions matter, these kids get a juvenile's viewpoint as an introduction to a very adult subject.

The critical missing link in the birds and the bees talk by parents is that the connection between sex and emotion is sorely left out, especially when parents talk to boys. The conversation is one viewed as the hardest and the most awkward to have between parents and kids, and this is the biggest problem.

Parents should have relationships with their children where either generation can bridge the gap and talk about anything at any time. Children need to hear this from a trusted source so that the necessary facet of sex is stressed, and it is not mistakenly framed as entertainment and objectification.

The conversation about sex should stress on the emotional facet of the act. Sex is not just about making babies. It's also about touching, bonding and uniting. Biochemical research in the area has identified the function of the various hormones that are released during the course of the sexual experience.

The conversation ideally should include a rational discussion about morality and the biology of the entire process and not just stop at the risk of pregnancy. Kids should also be warned about the other kids who peddle sensationalist views of reality. It's also important to discuss respect and love, as well. Boys, as much as girls, need to be taught self-worth.

Porn usually starts at a young age because of the ascendance and predominance of explicit scenes on the screen these days. Much of the skin that is consumed by pre-teens and teenagers is served up in music videos, video games, TV and websites. Commercial advertisements also use sex to persuade and attract, creating a time bomb in improperly socialized adolescents.

The route different people take to an addiction is as varied as the lives they lead. However, there are a few common paths that parents and social support groups can safeguard.

***

# Chapter 2: The Brain On Porn

*"Like an electric tea-kettle, pornography comes to a boil very fast."* ~ Mason Cooley

WHAT MOST PEOPLE THINK ABOUT porn couldn't be further from the truth. One of these misconceptions is that porn cannot harm the person watching it. This is not entirely true. Pornography damages the physical brain and alters its health. A scan of a brain addicted to porn reveals that the image is similar to that of an alcoholic's brain.

To understand the brain's response to porn addiction, we need to look at the cocktail of hormones that are released in the brain and body during a sexual experience. Mostly, the cocktail is similar between the genders, varying only in levels of each.

The human species is designed to unite two people to reproduce the next generation. It is nature's mixing bowl. With this requirement, genes combine with greater variability over time giving progressive generations better chances of adapting.

Nature doesn't really care about who the two people are who come together to create the offspring. It can be any two. There are two specific areas of bonding and attraction between the genders. The first is intellectual attraction through common values and shared visions; the other is physical attraction where physical attributes play a prominent role. Both lead to the coupling of the partners and sex is designed to have two outcomes.

First, of course, to create offspring. Second, it creates a bond between two people to allow them to become a good team, effective parents, and to be a support system to each other as they age. The argument to confirm the reason is speculative, but the consequence of the hormones is definitive. A definite bond is created upon its release in sexual encounters. The hormone and the body don't know how to distinguish what's in front of them. All it knows is to create intense memories, and thereby a strong bond with it.

In a human relationship, repeated sexual encounters with the same person result in the strengthening of the bond between two partners. (But all it takes is one sexual encounter to create this bond.) In a consumer-porn relationship, the bond is formed with the pornographic material.

Two of the hormones that are responsible for this, is the ubiquitous Dopamine, and the lesser known Norepinephrine. Dopamine increases craving, along with focus, while inducing euphoria that the mind remembers - leading to habits; while Norepinephrine is like adrenaline, except it's for the brain - it charges the brain up and gets it ready for activity.

In sex between couples, another chemical that is released is the hormone Oxytocin. Oxytocin is primarily responsible for bonding the two participants. When sex is between two adults who are in love, this is the root of bonding. The chemical creates the body to a deep acceptance of another individual and repeated exposure to the hormone in the presence of the same individual can create lifelong partnerships. However, Oxytocin also cannot decipher if the counterpart is a human or a porn flick. After repeated exposure, the viewer actually creates a bond with the flick.

Aside from the bond, the viewer is also forming a habit of going to porn for his entertainment, social needs, and biological urges. Porn starts to seem like a no-hassle guarantee that is always available. Between the convenience, the variety, and the satisfaction of increasing levels of sophistication and/or depravity, there is something for everyone; every possible fantasy that the viewer's mind can concoct. At this stage, porn can unknowingly become the perfect mate, effectively displacing the human partner/spouse.

Once the engagement is over, a different set of hormones is produced, first, endorphins for the high, and finally, serotonin, to relax the body. (Relaxing together after intercourse is an important part of the bonding process and the body secretes the serotonin for this purpose. We are wired to bond with a partner, not a computer screen. We are wired to be in relationship, not to be isolated.)

This cocktail of hormones is highly pleasurable and thus, highly addictive. A porn addict is actually addicted to these pleasures, but the trigger becomes pornography. The bonding is with the porn, the object of the pleasure. There are five stages in the typical addiction process, and they will be covered in the next chapter.

***

# Chapter 3: The Psychology of Pornography

*"I don't like to degrade women, but I like pornography."* ~ Lupe Fiasco

THIS COCKTAIL OF HORMONES is highly pleasurable and thus, highly addictive. A porn addict is actually addicted to these hormone-induced rewards, but, again, the trigger is the pornography. And as silly as it sounds, the bonding has been created with the porn, the object of the pleasure.

There are five stages in the typical addiction flight, as follows:

## Stage 1

It starts with earlier than usual exposure to sex. The hype of sex above and beyond what it really is can sometimes lead younger boys to force themselves into it just to be cool. It's like picking up cigarettes. It's the 'you're not cool if you haven't' situation. So, boys pick up the nerve to either watch porn, watch porn to know what to do (using it as a teaching aid) and try to engage in sex at an age that is often too early. The rejection rate at an early age is, of course, very high, that's if they even muster the courage to attempt it. Instead, porn offers an easy alternative and after a few encounters, they get more and more comfortable with watching it.

## Stage 2

This is the onset of addiction, and we're only at Stage 2. Addiction to the sensation, after the session, is only part of the story. The dulled mind is woken by the surge of dopamine at the onset of watching porn and the watcher feels alert. The alert feeling is a welcome change to the constant lethargy that begins to develop in a person at the cusp of porn addiction.

The irony is that the very cause that is responsible for the lethargy offers a solution with the Dopamine and Norepinephrine release. The sudden sharpening of senses makes the viewer believe that it is the best cure for his 'porn hangover'. It's like having a stiff drink the morning after binge drinking to cure a hangover. It just tightens the noose of addiction.

During this stage, they are increasingly detaching from their partner or spouse. Even if they are in bed with their partner, they often fantasize about something they watched. This has an effect on the couple's bedroom relationship initially, then gradually flows over to their everyday relationship as well, as they become more reclusive and despondent. They are also not as emotionally available. A lot of energy and emotional stature has been expended on pornography leaving less for the spouse and family.

## Stage 3

Once addiction takes hold, the first few months (sometimes years) is spent in escalation. Escalation happens because current levels of stimulation, over time, prove insufficient for the same level of arousal. It's like getting immune to alcohol. When alcoholics first start, just two cocktails and they are effectively inebriated. With time, the body desensitizes, and it takes a whole lot more to get to that initial effect. But with porn, desensitizing causes the addict to increase his stimulation in order to get the same kick.

At first, it may just be an increase in frequency, then an increase in duration, followed by an increase in the intensity of the graphics. Simple acts won't provide the same arousal it once did, and the person may turn to hardcore. From the increase in intensity, it proceeds to forms of fetishes that have underpinnings in the viewer's unique psychology. By this point, most of the addicts are already starting to exhibit degradation in social life as well as quality of daily life.

This escalation is usually the final straw that splits a marriage or at least splinters it. The addict's increasing preference for these fetishes is not reciprocated by the spouse. They are also not as emotional, or caring, and may even begin to want to act out what they've seen in porn movies. The movies mostly depict women as sexual objects and subservient to men's desires, no matter how depraved. In some cases, porn also instills, incorrectly, that women are secretly craving the same sexual experience. Of course, this is not the complete truth.

Women who give in often feel shame afterward. Women who do not give in can become angry and frustrated and feel as though they are not enough. Both, the ones who acquiesce and the ones who don't, are bewildered by the 'sudden' change in their partner's sexual appetite, preferences and unusual lack of warmth. Whatever vestiges of matrimony are left can erode at this stage.

## Stage 4

This is when nothing else will cut it any longer. The person is now almost fully desensitized and very few porn flicks, no matter how new or different, can provide satisfaction. At this point, the mind can become filled with aggression from the withdrawal of dopamine and all the other hormones that have been keeping them going.

There is an additional facet to this as well. The porn that they bonded to in the beginning, as though it was a partner, now begins to disappoint. Because of this, their frustration with the opposite sex is also at an all-time high and they may tend to blame them for the ills in their life.

Between the increase in this fetish, and the reduction of respect for women (way past the mere objectification) the logical step to the desensitization caused by porn, is now to act out the trove of sexual acts they have witnessed in their earlier stages of addiction.

In many cases, you find men gravitating towards prostitutes, and meaningless one-night stands. But this is the least harmful of all, because the next step, which follows soon after is the acting out of fetishes, and in many cases, prostitutes will not oblige, and neither will one-night stands.

Unfortunately, although uncomfortable to talk about, studies show this can lead to rape because of multiple motivations. (Frustration can turn to anger, then rage.) The first is that they are not getting what they want from willing partners, and the second is that rape is the aggregate of hostility and sex. It is a plausible progression for the pornography addict if they don't stop or get help.

Of course, by this point, their lives are already in disarray. Marriages and unions are over at this point with little to no chance of reconciliation.

## Stage 5

This is the final stage before implosion. The acting out gets serious and they either start running afoul and breaking the law, or they start to combine destructive behaviors. The two most common at this stage are alcohol and drug abuse. The impairment of their senses deepens further. A combination of reduced mental capacity from the erosion of gray matter caused by excessive dopamine, followed by the effects of drugs and alcohol add to the rage that has developed, disillusion becomes reality as they become self-destructive and have less and less to lose.

In Ted Bundy's case, and in his own words, hard-core pornography had provided the 'fuel for his fantasies." Charming Ted Bundy was a serial killer and rapist. He confessed to over 30 homicides, but some speculate there were hundreds of victims. Ted Bundy said pornography played a big role in the crimes that he committed.

Thankfully, many pornography addicts don't go this far, but their lives do tend to crumble and deteriorate slowly. Especially in the relationship department.

## The Physical Effects

Purely psychological effects can be regulated with some success through discipline, medication, and therapy. However, the problem with porn addiction, if not caught in time, is the erosion of grey matter which can, at times, be irreversible.

The physical degradation of the brain severely impacts the psychological attempt to intervene. The recovery process can be laborious and complex because there are many adverse consequences that have already manifested. Other addictions may be involved, aggression may be advanced and even a changed perspective of life could hinder the self-motivation needed for a cure.

We need to understand that every session in front of a porn flick has the potential to begin the cascade that results in the Five stages above. Awareness is key.

***

# Chapter 4: The World We Live In

*"It is not pornography that is obscene, it is hunger that is obscene."* ~ Jose Saramago

IN YEARS PAST, tradition and values of class and tact made the advertisement of explicit sexual material such as those which pornography is based upon, something unwelcome to the public. Yet, as times have changed such material has become freely available and even encouraged by most of society. Even technology has made pornography more widespread than it has ever been. The internet provides a well-known platform for pornography distribution that also allows partakers to remain completely anonymous; should they so choose under normal circumstances. There are over twenty-six million sites that host pornographic content and that number is growing by the day.

Every moment in time the combined traffic of all twenty-six million websites is no less than twenty-nine thousand people worldwide. While that may not at first seem significant, when taken into consideration that this is considered the minimum, you can imagine during prime hours of entertainment that figure grows exponentially. Males are believed to be 66% of those 29,000 and are generally believed to be a majority of the porn industries consumers.

According to figures released by the pornography industry, they claim to have made a stunning $97 billion worldwide in 2006. This figure is believed to be a slight exaggeration, however, as that would put the industry's revenue higher than all of the leading technology companies combined. Yet, there is no debate to commerce experts everywhere that the porn industry has churned out massive numbers of profit in recent years and only seems to be growing.

In older fashioned films it was uncommon to find a scene that was displayed on-screen or in front of an audience that even had a man and wife sharing a bed together. Such acts were often regarded with sanctity and privacy by a majority of society. Yet, change has proven itself to be the only constant throughout time and this is certainly the case with the standard of sexual images in everyday media. Sexually explicit images can be found in all forms of expression such as advertisements of all kinds, TV, music, and books.

Not only has the face of pornography changed, so too has the mindset behind it. In today's time, many see porn styled sexuality such as bondage as an alluring and even necessary aspect of intimacy. If you don't believe it then merely look at the success of *50 Shades of Grey*. The books prime theme was based upon a sexual relationship. It sold 125 million copies across the globe and has even made its way to the big screen as a major motion picture. Our day to day lives are seeing an increasingly large portion of them involved in explicit content in some way or another. Even emails have begun to spit out pornographic content at an astounding rate of 2.5 billion emails a day.

As times change so must we. We acknowledge that the subject of sexuality is no longer a taboo one and is instead quite openly considered. Yet, that doesn't mean this trend in media should follow into our personal lives. If we aren't questioning the involvement of today's accepted sexual norms in our relationships, then we most certainly should be. Relationships are already heavily stressed thanks to the world's fast-paced attitude; they don't need a lack of intimacy plaguing them as well.

# Chapter 5: What the Research Shows

*"Openness, respect, integrity - these are principles that need to underpin pretty much every other decision that you make." ~ Justin Trudeau*

## The majority of women are unhappy about their partner's pornography habits

RESEARCH HAS BACKED UP reports that young women with romantic partners who partake in pornography regularly are reportedly less happy in their relationships than women who are partnered with men who abstain from it. Some of these negative emotions are contributed to the feelings of inferiority women can develop while comparing themselves to the image norms portrayed through pornography. Research indicates that the pornography itself doesn't necessarily cause the insecurity, rather, it seems to compound already existing insecurities.

## Is Pornography Similar to Cheating?

Studies have often shown women to be more sensitive to the intricacies of infidelity than men. One study has shown that 36% of women believe pornography usage to be the same, in spirit, as cheating. Compare that to only 7% percent of men who feel the same way and you can begin to see the discrepancies between male and female beliefs about pornography. Further, 40% of women surveyed also revealed they frequently feel that their partner's usage of porn stems from sexual dissatisfaction. Women worry it is a sign of sexual boredom and that they no longer satisfy their partner. This shows that porn usage can cause unspoken tension between a couple, as many women feel discouraged (rather than encouraged) by their partner's behavior and pornography use.

## Unrealistic Expectations

Pornography has set a new standard in its industry for those who star in it. The films and images often seen in the porn industry are those of only select models who possess bodily proportions that are wholly unrealistic for the vast majority. This new standard has also changed the perceptions of men who view porn on a regular basis. As men become accustomed to being visually stimulated in this way and associate their pleasure with a woman who has such dimensions, they often unintentionally hinder the intimacy between themselves and their future partners, by subconsciously attempting to rationalize this new standard in their normal lives. Unfortunately, it's not realistic. Many don't fully understand or realize that technology (editing and filtering) has come into great play when it comes to these images and films. They allow visuals that are unreproducible in real life and set relationships up to ultimately fail when they simply can't meet the demands these new standards places upon them.

## What the Brain Does

Pornography addiction is on the rise and is easily explained by a comparison to drug addiction. While, of course, the two appear different in just about every aspect, the way the brain responds to the two of them in order to encourage particular behavior has been studied extensively. Pornographic images stimulate the man's visual cortex which then alerts the mind to jumpstart its mesolimbic system. The mesolimbic system is meant to encourage behavior by rewarding the mind with the release of dopamine, which causes a sense of feel-good euphoria in the brain. The brain also performs the exact same set of actions when drugs, such as cocaine, are introduced to the body. This quite literally forms an addiction; not necessarily to the substance, in this case, the pornographic image, but the rewarding rush of dopamine throughout the mind after the stimulus of the image is detected by the mind.

## Sexual pleasure decreases with increased pornography use

Pornography doesn't just set a new standard when it comes to the images couples associate with intimacy, however. It also places a new value on sexual performance that drastically changes the chemistry of sex. The porn industry takes those with the proper body proportions and portrays them as professional sex machines with an endless amount of sexual desire.

Yet this new standard has been shown to negatively affect relationships. A close examination of couples has proven that constant pornography usage begins to take away the spark of excitement that naturally comes with sex. As a porn user feels no feelings of love or companionship while browsing the pornographic content, he/she similarly train themselves to also keep a hard lock on their passionate feelings when sharing intimacy with partners. This undoubtedly hampers the passion of the moment and in the long term has been shown to decrease sexual pleasure and adversely affect the overall well-being of the relationship.

The body also shows a resiliency to pornography use similar to that of its ability to build up a tolerance to drugs. As drug users become more acclimated to whatever drug they are introducing to the body, their body will, over time, become trained in its resistant to the unnatural substance and larger doses are required to obtain the same effect. This is also true for porn use as the dopamine rewards slowly decrease over time as the mind begins to train itself for the stimulus it is receiving from the pornographic content. Thus, this leads to users dedicating increasingly more of their time to the habitual use of porn and are frequently needing to find more extreme sexual imagery in order to continue stimulating themselves.

## Where Does Choice Come In?

It's easy to become drawn into habitual porn usage and not as easy to discern how to distance oneself from it. This is due mainly to chemical changes that occur inside the body when an orgasm is attained. As most people are prone to self-pleasuring themselves through masturbation (or by finding a sexual partner to pleasure them during the watching of porn) simply due to the fact that visual stimulation alone is rarely, if ever, enough for one to orgasm.

During orgasm, Oxytocin is naturally released in order to closer bond you to the sexual partner you are deriving pleasure from. This is originally a survival instinct of the body to bind a man and women together in order for them to jointly have an invested interest in each other's safety and consequently the safety of their future child/children. This occurs due to Oxytocin's bonding properties as a hormone. Yet, as you can imagine, sexual pleasure during pornographic use is largely due to the images upon a screen, which, obviously, cannot be treated as a real partner would, of course, be treated. This can wreak havoc upon the internal processes associated with an orgasm and can blind one to the negative impacts the porn use could be having in their lives due to their dependence upon the feel-good dopamine and the bonding hormone, Oxytocin.

## Your script is literally being written for you

"Sexual script theory" is a relatively new term developed by psychologists in order to better explain that what we are visually taught as a definition of normal sex, becomes our realistic expectation of the act. As the images we view the explicit content on is often the form of a screen, the user slowly begins to see a literal "script" in their head of how sex should normally be carried out. The pornographic content is actually quite literally brainwashing you into believing that it's exactly how normal sexual interactions should truly be.

Younger users, of course, are affected much more by this phenomenon than those who are more experienced in sexual encounters. If one's first sexual experience is that of porn, then they are, of course, much more likely to see that as the typical standard and are more prominent to allowing that standard to influence their sexual expectations.

Those who set their pornographic standards to such a point are found more likely to attempt to replicate the scenes which they see bringing pleasure through a screen. Naturally many, if not all, fall short of the carefully choreographed videos that sometimes take porn stars' hours upon hours of filming to get just right. Most fail to realize all the work that goes into lighting, special effects, and off the screen coaching in order to make the films as sexually appealing as they can and when the real acts fall short many don't realize it's this unrealistic standard set by porn that is truly to blame.

Mainstream porn has been universally agreed upon by researchers that the materials are often "overwhelmingly centered on acts of violence and degradation toward women." Most mainstream pornography doesn't include the many normal forms of fondness and tenderness that are so needed to help develop healthy and loving relationships.

Note: This "norm" set by porn has been increasingly proven not to affect those with lower pornographic use. Those who do not watch porn simply aren't influenced by what would be considered a new standard and find that the exploration of their intimacy with their partners is increasingly more profound when explored without an outside influence. Just because pornography sets standards and "scripts" doesn't mean that's the natural flow of things and the intimacy of your relationship is entirely in your own control, not that of some porn film director.

**Decreased commitment to partners**

Many studies and research have reported concerns that increasing porn usage will negatively affect relationships in the coming years. The largest concern is in the field of infidelity. Many studies confirm that the social and psychological changes incurred by habitual porn usage clearly decrease commitment towards long-term partners. The behaviors of those who were more acclimated to porn use were found to be increasingly more at risk of flirting with outside partners and even involving themselves in a potentially relationship-ruining affair.

Pornography use has often been associated with those who believe their partners to be unfaithful and who feel as though their partner is the largest threat to their relationship's continued stability. Porn usage is also associated with increasing the likelihood of divorce in relationships and is increasingly being seen as a cause for separation.

Pornography usage doesn't just degrade your current relationships; it has also been proven to be a cause of dissatisfaction in future relationships, as well. In men with habitual pornography use, they've been found to be much less sensitive to their partner and less attuned to their needs. For women, pornography usage can lead to decreased self-confidence and a shift in the woman's behavior in an attempt to become more like what is seen in porn.

In addition, modern research now suggests that pornography no longer "objectifies" women. It instead "animalifys' them and leads to a degradation in the minds of all involved.

## Loss of interest in sex with your partner

Research done on couples has shown that 68% of relationships where one or even both persons was addicted to pornography usage has a drastic decrease in interest in lovemaking. This is mainly due to the fact that porn is being used to fulfill physical needs instead of looking towards one's partner. Porn also strays one's mind towards the variety of sexual partners available out there and weakens the resolve and commitment towards one's actual partner.

## Does Pornography Use Lower Commitment?

Many would argue that pornography usage has no direct link to the commitment felt between couples. Yet findings have reported otherwise, especially when it comes to pornography usage by men. Experiments have been given to test the intimacy and level of connection between couples. This was done by taking a group of couples and blindfolding one. The other partner was then required to give detailed instructions in order for the blindfolded one to draw an image. It was noted by observers that those who reported watching explicit material had a significantly harder time at the task.

Another study was done in order to determine the short-term differences between abstinence from pornography use and the commitment between couples. A group of couples was divided in half, with the first half pledging to abstain from sexually explicit material while the second half promised to give up their favorite food yet were still allowed to view porn. After three weeks the group that abstained from pornography saw a remarkable increase in their commitment to their relationship.

Several other studies have also observed the effects of how pornography usage affects the attention one dedicates toward their partner. Those who use pornography are reportedly more likely to also engage in flirting. This chance is exponentially increased if both (straying) partners are engaging in pornographic use. Studies show that the chance for infidelity is significantly higher than those who abstain from pornographic use.

The National Foundation for Family Research and Education at the University of Calgary decided to analyze 46 separate studies and found that regular exposure to explicit material not only affected the psychological nature of intimacy, but they also found it had a direct link to the age of one's first sexual (intercourse) encounter and had a tendency to lead towards excessive masturbation. Negative pornographic standards were also found, in the studies, to encourage aggressive rape-like behavior and even led women who regularly viewed extreme porn to believe these acts of sexual expression are okay.

These findings are also supported by neurological imaging studies done by Susan Fiske, a professor of psychology at Princeton University. By using MRI scans to analyze the brain activity of men watching pornography she was able to distinguish that men looked at women more as objects for pleasure during the viewing than as actual human beings.

## Pornography and Intimacy

Research suggests that pornography leads to a fear of intimacy or closeness also known as aphenphosmphobia. Men especially were proven to use porn as a replacement for real intimacy. This would support theories that those who use pornography aren't necessarily attempting to replace real intimacy, they are instead actually searching for intimacy, yet are afraid of the emotional attachments that come with committed relationships.

Pornography usage can be a contradictory subject for many psychologists. It is believed that many who turn to pornographic material for intimacy fulfillment are actually just missing real intimacy in their lives. They turn to the porn industry to attempt to fill the void that they aren't receiving from a partner. This is no fault of the partner; it is often due to fear or negative experiences intimacy caused in the past. In a case by case basis, it can be hard to determine the true cause that pushes one to use porn, and if it's not clearly evident what the origin of your specific situation is then a trained therapist is always a great option.

Therapists are trained to recognize patterns in behavior and reports from therapists all around the world indicate that the people who are most prone to pornographic addiction are those who may have received little to no love in their earlier lives. Those who come from love deficient households or environments were predisposed to the addiction that comes along with pornographic use because they simply never witnessed or experienced the real version of intimacy to the full extent.

## What Do Women Get Out of Pornography?

Women and men have differing subconscious reasons that draw them towards pornography. Women are more likely to attempt to involve their partners in their pornographic use as women often see porn as a way to enhance their intimacy. Pornographic use by women is often commonly associated with an exploration of their sexuality, while this is, of course, not a set-in-stone rule it tends to be more often than not true.

Men, when they are mentally aroused through the visual cues given by porn, are also physically aroused as their two sexual identities, mental and physical, are closely related. In women, however, many find that when they are mentally aroused, through visual stimulation, that their bodies remain unaroused until more direct action is taken. Men are also able to obtain orgasm more often than women, especially when it comes to masturbation and self-pleasure. This leads men to commonly self-pleasure themselves with porn nearly 50% of the time they are engaging in its use, according to studies performed by the Archives of Sexual Behavior. Yet, women only use porn as a self-stimulating tool on an average of 9% of the time.

Women are more prone to using erotic literature in substitute for pornographic use. Erotica displays an unrealistic standard to women much like porn does for men. Women find their relationship views and expectations are sometimes changed and influenced by erotica. Women who read increasingly more erotica have been found to, at times, have unrealistic standards for their relationships as they expect their days to be filled with fantasy, excitement, and passion.

Erotica is often seen more positively by researchers than pornographic use. Erotic literature seems a bit more morally correct than pornography. As the use of it can help spice up the couple's bedroom life without setting differing standards that could cause isolation or separation. The relationship standards are often set higher by erotica and cause couples to strive to improve their relationship which tends to cause an increase in communication between partners.

## When It's Unhealthy

A majority of men and women control their pornographic use, however. Many realize, as they become older, that the intimacy provided by porn is, of course, synthetic and can't stand up to the real thing. Therefore, their pornographic habits tend to be in trends. Increases are shown when one is single, under increased stress, or their partner is absent. But when the situation (that makes their real intimacy unavailable) is resolved, a majority of them would much rather prefer real intimacy over anything porn could provide them.

Unfortunately, a small percentage (3-5%) of pornographic users find themselves addicted to the arousal porn offers. These people turn toward pornography in order to help emotionally stabilize themselves. Some even use it for a means of comfort or to reduce anxiety. For them, the usage of porn is much more serious and can lead to long-term damages to their standards of intimacy and even lead some to lie to others about their pornographic habits.

The biggest issue many observe in relationships when it comes to pornography tends not to be the recreational usage of it. Many, instead, see secret pornographic usage as the biggest issue. As with any secret, it may eventually come out and when it does your partner is likely to feel betrayed, at least in some small way.

A study has explored the nature of the different ways pornography affects the perceptions of a person and influences their wants and desires. In some, the visual stimulation of physically attractive and sexually accepting partners on-screen can impact that person's views upon their current or future partners. And, a second possibility is that it can introduce the concept of multiple sexual partners to someone and begin leading them down a road that could ultimately destroy any committed relationship.

Another study shows that those who partake in pornographic content often are more likely to see their current partners as replaceable. The actors in porn movies switch partners easily and often.

And finally, another study shows that pornographic usage predisposes one to become more likely to contemplate cheating on their partners.

These studies focus on the fact that it isn't necessarily dissatisfaction that leads to this behavior. It's merely the seed of thought implanted by the world of porn. When one thinks of other possible partners or feels the impulses to find those partners, they are merely reacting to what porn encourages and reinforces; exploration of sexual pleasure and less emphasis upon the intimacy and bond the act naturally creates.

## Frequency

Research also shows links between the frequency of pornographic use with those who are able to detach themselves intimately from their partners. The longer one uses porn the less they see their partner as a need or desire. Psychologists and researchers have agreed that when one is increasingly stimulated by porn on a regular basis, they begin to experience an increase in sexual objectification of strangers or to those they have no emotional bond with. Similar to the fact that one doesn't know those who are in the sexually explicit material, they also don't know the strangers they pass in day-to-day life. Porn is not like a romance movie where the characters ultimately build a relationship, fall in love and eventually get together. In porn, the characters are clearly strangers and have no emotional attachment. As time goes on the viewer begins to associate that no intimate bonds need to be built in advance before the sexual act takes place. Often this behavior is reversible when one decreases their use of porn. It's much like a sliding scale that is increasing and decreasing based upon the frequency of pornographic use.

Some may scoff at this idea, because we all know right from wrong, yes? I've had people say, "just because I watch something doesn't make me thinks it's okay". But it's now common knowledge that what you feed your brain, has a huge impact on one's life. The brain rewires itself by what we consistently feed it. My book on Neuroplasticity covers more of how this works. The more you do something, the more the brain adapts and accepts it.

Therefore, frequency of porn use clearly matters.

## Is pornography in the bedroom ever ok?

Pornography can help couples become more familiar with their sexual desires. It has allowed many couples the ability to increasingly voice their desires and to become more comfortable in a more sexual environment. Nearly 25% of men and women say pornography has helped them be more open to experimenting in the bedroom and psychologists have agreed that pornography can help advance sexual learning. Yet someone who is depressed or lonely is at an increased risk for compulsive sexual behavior.

A study published in the journal Psychology of Addictive Behaviors showed that those who sought out pornography for sexual education experienced positive changes in their real-life sexual activity. But those who sought out pornography in order to cope with stress or depression reported increased relationship issues instead. As with many things, the difference is merely in the intent of the action.

For many who become addicted to pornography, the issues aren't always related to sexual desires or intimacy. They can also often originate from chaotic events in life that have caused negative connotations to develop themselves. Pornography then becomes a fantasy where one can feel good about themselves and find a release from the stress of their past experiences.

Couples who reported using sexual media together, to grow their intimacy, revealed higher relationship satisfaction than those who instead turn towards porn alone. This would support and explain how couples who use pornographic material together can sometimes experience positive results. Scientists have warned, however, that this isn't an encouragement for sexual media usage for couples. They're merely claiming that sexual enjoyment of explicit material together is less likely to harm your relationship with your partner or spouse than the use of the same material alone.

***

# Chapter 6: Facts to Make You Think

*"It's possible to be pro-sex and anti-pornography."* ~
*Gloria Steinem*

THE FOLLOWING FACTS about U.S. and international pornography usage have not been verified for the current year, but there is enough evidence backing them and more than enough credibility to require these facts to be considered and introduced to the masses.

- Over 68 million searches for pornography are made daily in the United States, this is nearly 25% of searches made in the U.S. (IFR, 2006).
- The sex industry is one of the most profitable in the world and includes a large range of services that doesn't merely stop at virtual pornographic use. The porn industry includes but is not limited to the following; street prostitution, brothels, 'massage parlors', strip clubs, human trafficking for sexual purposes, phone sex, child and adult pornography,

mail order brides and sex tourism. (Andersson et al, 2013).

- 13% of global web searches in 2010 were for sexual content. (Ogas $ Gaddam).

- Pornographyhub, a large destination for pornographic users, receives over 1.68 million visits PER HOUR. (pornographyhub, 2013).

- Globally 'teen' is the most searched term. When it comes to pornography 'teen pornography' was the fastest growing genre showing a drastic increase, more than tripling, between 2005 and 2013. In March of 2013, an estimated half a million searches daily were made for teen related pornography. (Dines, 2013)

- The United States is the largest producer of pornographic DVD and web material. The second largest country for pornographic material development is Germany. Both countries produced an excess of 400 original pornographic films for DVD every week.

- Internet pornography in the UK receives more online traffic than social networks, shopping, news, email, finance, gaming, and travel.

- Several studies have also reported that teenagers around the world admit that they use pornography regularly for sexual education and information about real-life sex. (Lauzus et al, 2007) (Wade et al, 2005) (Flood, 2009) (Giordano & Ross, 2012).

- Several studies have reported that women on average watch pornography much less than men.

- Condoms have only been utilized in 10.9% of top-rated pornographic materials (Bridges and Wosnitzer, 2007).

- In 2006, 10% of adults admitted to believing they have an addiction to online pornography. (IFR, 2006).

- In the United States alone, every 39 minutes a new pornography film is produced.

- 20% of American men have admitted to accessing porn while at work.

- 70% of all internet pornography traffic occurs during normal working hours on workdays (9am-5pm, Monday-Friday) (Sex Tracker, 2012)

- Companies have reported that 2/3 human resource professionals in the U.S. have found pornography on employee's work computers. (Paintbottle, 2013).

- Recent studies reveal that nearly seven of ten youth have been exposed to pornography in the U.S. unwillingly. (Carroll et al, 2008).

- Children as early as 11 are regularly exposed to hardcore gonzo pornography. (IFR, 2006).

- The largest consumer group of internet pornography is commonly boys between the ages of 12-17 after their first exposure.

- 88.2% of all top-rated pornographic scenes contain aggressive and abusive acts.

- 70% of aggressive occurrences that occur in porn is begun by a man. In 94% of these cases, a woman is the one being degraded by the act.

- Only 9.9% of the top-selling scenes contained intimate behaviors such as kissing, laughing, caressing, or complimenting.

- Open handed slapping is the most common form of aggressive behavior in porn and occurs in 41.4% of scenes.

- Sex in pornography is mainly focused upon sexual pleasure and orgasm for the male rather than equal pleasure for both partners. (Bridges and Wosnitzer, 2007).

- Pornography is diversified often into various stereotypical and demeaning categories for actors. These genres can be based upon ethnicity, age, body type, or even sexual experience.

- Almost 20% of all internet pornography is sexual abuse on children. (National Center for Missing and Exploited Children, 2013).
- Studies have shown that after viewing porn men are more likely to:
  - experience decreased empathy for rape victims
  - experience increasingly aggressive behavioral patterns
  - believe women who dress provocatively deserve any sexual mistreatment they get

- report having anger towards women who flirt then refuse to take it further sexually
- decreased sexual interest in spouses or long-term partners
- report increased frequency and manipulation of partners into unwanted sex acts (Bridges, 2006) (Yang, Gahyun, 2012).

• The pornography industry makes significantly more money than Hollywood. (U.S. Statistics)

• Annually over 13,000 adult videos are produced and amass over $13 billion in profit. Hollywood in comparison only released 507 movies to make $8.8 billion in 2007. (Bridges and Wosnitzer, 2007)

• The porn industry also makes more than top technology companies such as Microsoft, Google, Amazon, eBay, Yahoo, Apple, and Netflix combined. (IFR, 2006)

***

# Chapter 7: Is Addiction to Pornography a Real Thing?

*"No one shuts their laptop after looking at pornography and says, 'What a productive time I just spent connecting with the world!"* ~ Russell Brand

AS TECHNOLOGY HAS MADE sexually explicit material and services more readily available, the porn industry has seen a tremendous increase in the use of online pornography in both men and women. Services such as Ashley Madison and other hook-up services have thrived as involvement has continually increased over the years. While for many this wouldn't be a problem but for those who are emotionally vulnerable or intimacy challenged, they may find themselves stuck in a habitual use of pornography that they simply can't break free from without dedicated effort.

Psychologists have set four stages or phases that define an addiction. (The Witherspoon Report)

1) **Addiction**, this results from the early on and repeated exposure to explicit content. It is further encouraged when masturbation is involved.

2) **Escalation**, as is seen with many drug addicts this is the stage where the body becomes used to the stimulus it is receiving and therefore requires more in order to reach a similar level of "high".

3) **Desensitization**, this is the stage where addicts will begin to consider sexual acts that would normally be repulsive or immoral as okay and acceptable.

4) **The acting out phase**, this is the phase where action viewed on media is transferred to real life actions such as abuse or even to the extreme of committing criminal acts such as rape.

Studies have shown that the acting out phase is by far the most damaging to those involved. People are more likely to participate in infidelity or even other immoral acts such as child pornography or molestation to find new ways to explore their sexuality. Those who have been unfaithful to their partners in some way have also been shown to be over 3 times more likely to have a habitual usage of online pornography.

For those who become addicted, the act is no longer one of mere curiosity but one of obsession. The addict finds that their need for the 'virtual' sex continues to grow. In order to avoid boredom, they must, of course, turn to more and more drastic measures over time.

As the sexual arousal increases in intensity, the addict's body becomes increasingly desiring of their next 'hit'. This includes nearly 8% of men and 3% of women in the U.S. who have become sexually addicted, with other studies claiming that at least 200,000 Americans are hopelessly addicted to online porn.

Sex between intimate partners develops over an extended duration and is completely different from sex based upon new experiences and intensity. As sex between intimate partners involves thoughts of the well-being of the couple as a whole, the thoughts are inherently much more positive and loving. But those who focus merely on the intensity of the moment, or living out fantasies, are much more likely to hurt one another.

Fantasies are called fantasies for a reason. They should remain there, because once they become reality, usually everything changes and not in a good way. (I have a perfect example of this from someone who submitted a testimony.)

## About Addictions

An addiction can be defined as any destructive behavior that becomes someone's way of coping with stress, pressure, or boredom. Some addictions are genetically passed down, but others, such as sexual addictions and eating disorders, tend to stem from physical, emotional, or sexual abuse.

Just because one is engaging in unhealthy behavior doesn't automatically make that behavior an addiction, but it does mean that that behavior can become an unhealthy addiction. It is vital then that when one is performing these unhealthy acts that they constantly take stock of their emotional health and assure that their situation isn't deteriorating into something uncontrollable.

## Psychologists believe addictions all share these traits:

### 1) Fantasy

Addiction is often a way for one to escape the hardships that come along in life. These can typically come in the form of an overstressed or overwhelmed person finding safety in a behavior or action and then becoming attached to that behavior or action in order to survive and escape. However, for an addict, the fantasy stops being an occasional thing and instead begins to take over that person's entire life. They begin to obsess over their addiction and find that they are trapped inside their own fantasy. The obsessions with their addiction can become so strong that psychological responses in the mind can even trigger bodily responses just at the thought of their weakness. This is even made easier when one is able to physically arouse themselves just by merely thinking of pornography.

### 2) Emotions

When a person finds themselves engaging in addictive behavior it is more often than not due to the triggering of strong emotions. These emotions bring temporary relief and happy and euphoric feelings which can consistently be returned by merely engaging in the fantasy once again. Many addicts turn to their fantasy merely for the control it gives them over their emotions as it allows them to constantly reward themselves by experiencing that emotional or physical high.

## 3) False Sense of Control

For many addicts, their fantasy comes back to the issue of control. While many can't control life's daily flow of stress and challenges, they can often turn towards their fantasy and feel in control. Many pornography addicts will turn towards using pornography in order to relieve stress instead of looking for healthier alternatives such as exercise. They often ignore whatever the actual origin is for their real-life stress.

## 4) Self-Nurturing

Addictive behaviors become more and more addictive over time as they increasingly continue to relieve the addict of the stresses they are attempting to cope with. The addiction becomes a harmful and false way to self-nurture oneself. It is a brief relief that is far more damaging than not.

## 5) Self-Destructive

Addictions are of course only negative when they become self-destructive. If one becomes addicted to doing something positive, then it tends to not be classified as an addiction merely due to the non-destructive nature. Yet with many addictions, such as pornography, the behavior is an embarrassing and often unsupported one that leads to self-loathing and self-punishment. The self-loathing causes the person to turn once again to their fantasy for comfort and it goes on in an endless cycle of self-loathing and gratification which leads to increased self-loathing and depression and destruction.

***

# Chapter 8: Why Couples Turn to Pornography

*"The real man smiles in trouble, gathers strength from distress, and grows brave by reflection." ~ Thomas Paine*

As MENTIONED PREVIOUSLY, many couples introduce pornography into their relationship in hopes of spicing things up in the bedroom. Some believe that this can be perfectly fine when it is done with the consent of both partners. If both partners are seeing the inclusion as a healthy new addition to their relationship and both partners truly enjoy the inclusion, then it can rekindle intimacy.

However, if the use of pornography begins to become obsessive and either partner begins to find themselves becoming less aroused by their partner, or even in general, then it's important that the subject is quickly addressed and discussed. Weigh the pros and cons. It may even be prudent to abstain from pornography use until the issue is resolved. As discussed in previous chapters already, studies show that there are far more cons than pros to pornography.

There could be other issues that need to be addressed as well. If the intimacy you're experiencing with your partner is diminished then porn might not be the answer, instead, look at these traits to see how else you can fix or improve your relationship.

### 1) Hurt, anger, or resentment

These feelings can often originate from long-standing and unresolved issues. They can come from issues between the two of you or even from outstanding issues from past relationships. The best way to resolve these things is to openly communicate with your partner and explore your feelings to see if there are any connections the two of you aren't making due to miscommunication.

### 2) The sex spark fades

Over time, sex may become a ritual that is followed to the T between partners. As the sex becomes more and more predictable, one or even both partners may begin to suffer from boredom and see the act more as a chore than something to look forward to.

### 3) Sexual problems

Sexual inabilities such as erectile dysfunction or difficulties achieving orgasm can greatly affect the healthy sex life of a couple. These can be even further compounded when compared to the standards set up by pornography.

### 4) Who initiates sex?

This can be a big and unspoken factor between couples. When one partner is consistently the one who attempts to initiate sex yet is repeatedly turned down then feelings can get hurt and some of the issues in the first point can begin to arise. Both partners should make an active effort to initiate sexual intimacy when appropriate and should attempt to have an equal stake in their sexual life.

## 5) Sex as a priority

Sex can often be pushed to the side when couples are tired after a long day. In today's fast paced times, it's easy to just simply make the excuse that there's no time for intimacy. When couples allow their intimacy to take a seat on the back burner, they are essentially placing their relationship second as well.

## 6) Laziness

As couples become more used to, and familiar with, one another they may stop seeing that little bit of extra effort they saw in the beginning. Couples also begin to allow their hygiene and appearance to fall short and even at times allow their sexual performance to be affected.

## 7) Not addressing sexual problems

Many couples avoid addressing issues, such as erectile dysfunction, and instead begin to avoid sex altogether. This can lead to shame and embarrassment by either partner and even cause unresolved tension.

## 8) Forgotten foreplay

Women particularly require foreplay in order to become sexually aroused and in order to better connect with their partners. Foreplay can also be in the form of flirting, undivided attention, affection, and touching, kissing, and caressing. As a woman is given foreplay her desire for a physical relationship can increase. Men, however, don't require foreplay nearly as much as their female counterparts and instead tend to rely upon sex as an act of love and appreciation and forget about foreplay altogether. As this is a discrepancy between the way the male and female minds work it can take a combined and constant effort to face this difference and overcome it.

If you are experiencing a diminished sex life with your partner any one of these above points could be part of the problem. A supportive approach is necessary to tackle all of these challenges and for most couples, it's easily doable. Many couples can handle these issues, without professional help if they are willing to put in the time and effort required.

***

# Chapter 9: Long Term Effects On Your Relationship

*"Experiences aren't pornographic; only images and representations - structures of the imagination - are."* ~ Susan Sontag

Based on many of the studies we already discussed, the long-term effects of using pornography have become quite clear and transparent. These attacks on intimacy can, unfortunately, be fatal to even the strongest of relationships.

**Damage to the relationship, happiness, and even life satisfaction**

Many people who seek help, for pornography addiction, report it is mainly due to the negative impact they have seen in their personal lives and relationships. Over 4,000 people in an online survey admitted to seeking help due to these negative effects upon their lives and the difficulty they experience in halting their pornographic use. Many of these people also report they believe their pornographic addiction is related to depression, anxiety, or loneliness.

Pornography, by it's very nature, causes one to focus on their own pleasure instead of focusing on building intimacy and love. This can cause people to unintentionally prioritize porn over things such as; marriage, careers, families, or even financial stability. And they don't even realize that they are doing it.

**Erosion of Trust**

Many relationships rely upon trust in order to function. Sex is often an intimate and trusting connection between two partners and anytime either partner invites others into the act it can hurt their partner or even cause feelings of betrayal. Even the inclusion of 'virtual' partners can develop rifts in the intimacy being formed and developed between the couple.

**Erosion of trust leads to separation**

When the trust between a couple begins to deteriorate it can often lead to a large variety of other relationship related issues that aren't just centered around the couple's intimacy. It can also cause a quick breakdown of the trust that has grown over time. This quick collapse can leave either partner feeling vulnerable or taken advantage of. Improper pornography usage can be one of the fastest ways to foster distrust in a loving relationship and can cause an extreme amount of hurt when one partner finds out the other is secretly addicted to porn.

**Triggering trauma**

Pornography can trigger past traumas. Those who have been sexually abused can be reminded of their traumatic past when introduced to some of the immoral and rougher parts of sexuality displayed in porn. This can also lead past victims to close themselves off from their partner if they believe their partner is enjoying or finding pleasure from the same material. This can further breed distrust amongst the couple and can even put the emotional well-being of one at risk.

**The search for emotional intimacy**

Emotional intimacy is the strongest long-lasting factor in a healthy and stable relationship. This is greatly developed during the healthy sex life of a couple. Yet if a couple's sex life is negatively impacted by one partner looking for sexual stimulation or entertainment outside of the relationship then the emotional intimacy can just as quickly be broken down and damaged.

# Chapter 10: The Core of Marriage and Family

*"How do I know pornography depraves and corrupts? It depraves and corrupts me."* ~ Malcolm Muggeridge

The sanctity of marriage is not a construct of religion or an idle belief. It is real and it is a fundamentally necessary part of our lives, as a person, as a member of society and as a species. Some believe that marriage (commitment) is the building block of the species. Every culture and religion take marriage's place in society seriously, and rightfully so.

But placing religion and culture as the cornerstone for the argument of the sanctity of marriage is insufficient. The sanctity of marriage goes beyond symbolic rituals and poetic utterances. Marriage is the fragile binding that temporarily holds the union of man and woman until the real bond between the two emerge and solidify.

The bond created by natural sexual relations in a monogamous relationship goes so much further than any prenuptial agreement, marriage contract, matrimonial license or wedding ritual could ever go.

The true bonds of marriage are not found in the wedding band but in the honest sexual relationship of the couple. The bond that forms during the early part of the union remains solidly intact even after all physical urge of sex dissipate in the aging body. A couple without this bond, find the road of the latter years harder to navigate.

Just as having extramarital affairs dilutes and erodes the bond between one man and one woman, pornography does the same, and more. The causes are not just illusory and psychological, they are real and measurable.

The bonds that form between a monogamous couple also form the foundation of becoming good parents. Parenting is not about providing gaming systems and pizza on demand. Parenting is about fostering the family home with love that permeates across good times and bad. It's not enough to love your kids, you have to love your spouse (and others around you) if you want your child to feel the power of life and love.

Fathering a child is not the same as being a father to a child. Being a father to a child also means loving and respecting that child's mother with unconditional and focused bonds. (Even parents who get divorced realize that maintaining a friendly and loving relationship benefits the children enormously.)

Pornography is the antithesis to true happiness, and it affects the viewer, their partner, and children if applicable. It has no place in one's life no matter how infrequent. Basically, nothing good can come from pornography addiction.

***

## Chapter 11: Creating Fulfilling and Rewarding Sexual Relationships

*"The physicality of a real relationship - one that encompasses mind, body, and soul - ultimately makes it more fulfilling and powerful than any virtual relationship ever could be."* ~ Henry Cloud

A HEALTHY AND ROMANTIC relationship often involves physical, intellectual, and emotional connections between the couple. Yet sometimes a balance needs to be found when any one of these various connections doesn't quite match up together.

Even when relationships undergo periods of decreased sexual activity it isn't usually the couple plans to abstain from sex for long. Sometimes, time just goes by, and before you know it days and weeks have passed. Many times, these sexual breaks can be difficult to reverse and can take some amount of time and effort to restore the sexual intimacy to bring it back to a comfortable and healthy level. But it has been done and it can be done! There are many ways to help rebuild the sexual intimacy of your relationship in the bedroom such as;

## 1) Communicate

If there isn't open communication occurring between couples, then it can become increasingly harder to get issues and tensions dispelled. Communication is also essential in one's sex life in order to convey a partner's desires or needs. While many of us can at times struggle to communicate our feelings and open up to our partners, it's important to at least attempt to convey our feelings to one another. It's also important to make the time to talk and communicate with consistently in order to help diffuse any problems or tensions between the couple as they arise in order to prevent them from festering. Asking questions can help initiate communication as well.

## 2) Quality Time

Many modern couples are always so busy that they hardly find quality alone time to spend together growing their bond. This quality time can be the simplest of things such as doing household tasks together or just holding one another for a few minutes before bed or in the morning each day. These small pockets of time spent together, can contribute immensely to the intimacy between the couple. The reason new relationships tend to be so powerful is due to the amount of time dedicated to learning and getting to know more about one another. The adventure of discovery between one another should never come to an end, and it doesn't have to. Make time out of your busy schedule to love on your partner.

## 3) Make gratitude a part of daily life

Many people feel like they aren't appreciated for everything they do on a daily basis. It's easy to tell your partner before bed that you're simply grateful for the things they have done for you each day. Always remember that life could be so much worse without that person in it and even something as simple as thanking someone for their presence in your life can bring a million-watt smile to your partner's face. Appreciation and gratitude go a long way.

## 4) Create some quick moments together

This can often accompany point number 2. Make a small daily habit, such as a walk around the corner while holding hands. Maybe have a small daily message of love you tell one another before heading off to work. Any small loving ritual, such as this, can begin to wear down on even the most hardened of barriers between a couple and the small extra effort it requires always becomes well worth it in the end.

## 5) Improve your listening

Many couples don't often truly listen to one another's issues. This comes with our hurried lifestyles because we often don't take the time it requires to be in the moment and truly pay attention to what our partner is saying. When you ask them things such as how their day has been, actually listen and analyze their response in order to pick up on anything they might not be vocalizing but are still expressing with their tone of voice. Also, make eye contact and be sure to pause to make sure that your partner is done speaking before you interrupt or begin to speak. These are good habits to get into to show that you are really listening and that you really care.

## 6) Show affection

Small displays of affection, such as a hug or the giving of a single rose along with a kiss, can really make your partners day. Open the door for them, pour them their favorite drink, buy them their favorite candy bar the next time you stop for gas or leave them little love notes to find throughout the day. These small signs of love and caring, over time, can have a massive effect on the dynamics of a relationship and can help drive home the simple message that you care. It can also reassure your partner that you're there for the long haul.

## 7) Rekindle the Past

Talk about your past with one another. Help each other understand childhood memories that might explain why you are the way you are about certain things. Or simply reminisce about happy memories you share with one another. This helps build a sense of mystery and it also helps keep the couple's attention upon positive thoughts and memories and off of stress or breaks in intimacy. Don't dwell on the past, rather, remember and reminisce about the good times.

## 8) Shower together

Bathe and shower together. It's a great time to have undivided attention and alone time. Some people are uncomfortable being seen completely naked, but intimacy is about being vulnerable and trusting. Dim the lights if you must, but more importantly, don't listen to any negative self-talk and enjoy yourself. The more you do it, the easier it will become. Couples who shower together on a regular basis maintain more intimacy and openness. Sex (including oral sex) is a lot of fun in the shower as well. You are warm, relaxed, clean, and smell good. And it's good for the environment because you'll save water, too. *Wink wink.

## 9) Restore intimacy through sensual touching

Sensual touching can be a great thing between couples, especially for women. Just simply enjoying the feel of each other with light and loving touches can help ease stress and convey love and affection without the need for actual sex. This can also help diffuse and ease couples into their sex life gently if there have been intimacy issues before in your sex life. Just touch each other in loving ways without any ulterior motives.

## 10) Kiss Like Teenagers

The French are known as people of love for good reason! Use that French Kiss like you mean it! This is one of my simplest pieces of advice, yet, it has the biggest impact. Don't believe me? Try it. And I mean really try it. Brush your teeth or stick a tic tac or mint in your mouth and make-out for five minutes straight. Set a timer if you need to. Or simply look at the time and go for it. It's a fun game and will enhance everything about your relationship. In the beginning of all relationships, kissing plays a big part. Think back for a minute. How often did you kiss when you first started dating? You can't help but feel close, not to mention "hot and bothered" by this display of affection. And you can't stay mad long either. It's fun and playful. Be sure to really kiss your partner at least once a day.

## 11) Flirt!

Flirting is one of the easiest ways to communicate positively with one another. The laughter and playfulness that can accompany flirting are lightening for both of you. Simple teasing and nice compliments between couples can help set a light mood and help both of you begin to foster a closer friendship.

## 12) Make time for sex

While spontaneous sex is no doubt fun, every couple should assure that they have plenty of time set aside for privacy and lovemaking. Find ways to make this routine spiced up instead of simply a scheduled meet up. Add in games, flirting, or even some surprises to mix things up. Whatever you do, though, make sure you never miss your sexy appointment with one another. Make each other a priority. If you had an appointment with a doctor, or your accountant, or even a scheduled lunch with a friend, you'd make sure you show up. This is no less important. Schedule this time. Recent research also indicates that couples should take turns initiating sex. It shouldn't just be one-sided. I've said it before, but I will say it again, in the beginning, you both made plans and created time and space to be together and have alone time. Don't stop now.

## 13) Set aside pornography

If you are a couple that consistently utilizes pornography, then try to set it aside for a time. See if a break from the porn will help rebuild your relationship and begin helping you break away from the habits and standards porn sets. Instead, spend that time watching your partner and see where things go. We've seen, from the research in previous chapters, that porn ultimately hinders everything, including our sex lives. Some of our clients report that after they stop viewing pornography their sex lives thrive. We've had many people state that pornography was the cause of their erectile dysfunction. They viewed pornography so much that they had a difficult time keeping an erection while they were with their partner (and not watching porn). This has nothing to do with the partner. No one is doing anything wrong. It has to do with the brain. When someone has been watching a lot of porn, the brain learns that that is what it takes to become aroused. Thankfully, this can be reversed with time. Stop the porn and in time your sex life, with an actual partner, will become better and better.

**14) Embrace focused sex therapy**

If your relationship is struggling to get back to where it once was or to even establish itself in the first place, then don't hesitate to seek out professional help. You'd be surprised to see what a few open-minded sessions with a professional or therapist can do to struggling intimacy. It can help us become aware of other avenues and ideas that we might not have thought about before.

\*\*\*

# Chapter 12: Testimonies

THE FOLLOWING ARE TRUE TESTIMONIES submitted by people whose lives have been affected, in one way or another, by pornography. I like to include testimonies from real people. It helps others relate, and I believe that we can learn from other people's mistakes. Some of these testimonies give examples from two different perspectives. We can learn from both. I wish I could share all of the testimonies that were submitted, and I thank everyone who shared their stories. My team and I picked a few testimonies that we thought others could relate to most.

**Testimony 1:**

Dear Sage,

Thank you for the opportunity to share my story. I hope that it can help others who may be in a similar situation. Talking with you and working through it has been an amazing adventure and I am very happy that you came into my path on this journey.

I am in my midlife years, and I was single for a long time. I tried several dating websites and just became more and more frustrated with it, that is until the day I decided to completely go off the last dating site I was a member of. That's it! I was fed up! I had had enough, and I logged in to cancel my membership. But before I did so, I could see that I had one message waiting to be opened. I opened it and it was from a gentleman who surprisingly lived in the same town that I did. (All of my previous dates had been at least 30 – 60 mins away, and here this guy was, and he lived literally five minutes from me.) So, reluctantly I agreed to meet him for coffee. Well, to say we hit it off would be an understatement. Our coffee date lasted three hours and I hadn't laughed so hard in ages. My face and stomach hurt from all the smiling and laughing I did.

We shared stories of our pasts and what had brought us to where we were. He had been single for several years as well. He had been married for 20 years until his wife passed away from a long-term illness. And he hadn't dated anyone since her death which was two years previous.

I continued dating this wonderful man and as the months rolled on things started getting more and more physical between us. One evening we ended up in the bedroom and decided we were more than ready to make love. Things went okay, but he was having trouble staying aroused, for a lack of a better description. But it was okay, it was our first go at it and he hadn't been with anyone in a long time. We could try again.

As we continued trying, the same thing kept happening. He was embarrassed because he wanted to please me, and I was just trying to help him not feel bad about it. Maybe it was a health issue? Maybe he needed to take one of those little blue pills I had heard about? We just weren't sure why it was happening. So, he made an appointment with his doctor who isn't a traditional doctor. He is a health guru doctor really, and the first thing he asked him was if he watched pornography on a regular basis. His answer, of course, was yes. He had been single for years, and he owned a computer, so it was easily available to him. He had been watching porn, and masturbating, on a regular basis for years, and he felt that he helped him relieve his stress and the grief even of his wife's passing.

His doctor told him that if he wanted to have a better sex life with me, then he would have to stop watching porn. (He also stopped masturbating in the shower.) It was that simple and his doctor wanted him to try it before he ran any blood tests or prescribed any medication for him.

Within four weeks (less than a month), we were having amazing sex. It worked! That was four years ago now and we are still having amazing sex and on a very regular basis. It's wonderful!

I can't believe the difference in our relationship and sex life once my man cut pornography out of his life. I also can't believe what a negative effect it can have on one's body. It was so frustrating, for both of us, that he couldn't stay aroused long enough for either of us to really enjoy each other. It's all in the brain and how powerful it is. Thankfully, we figured it out without medication which I am told can only add to the frustration.

Wishing everyone a blessed journey,

Hannah M.

## Testimony 2

I am a 38-year-old mother of three beautiful children. My husband works a lot and when my children all started going to school during the day, I found myself exploring different erotic websites. It started with erotic literature. I mean, reading erotic stories isn't all that bad, is it? It's literature. It's art, I kept telling myself. Of course, on these sites, there are also links and images and video clips of other things such as porn sites. It is a bit addicting. You see one thing and click on it, and then another and click on it. It starts with curiosity. I remember clicking on one site and it was a loving couple fondling each other and making sweet sensual love. It was beautiful and I secretly wished my marriage was like that. And then I masturbated and pleasured myself and then later picked up the kids and made dinner and got them ready for bed and gave my husband a quick peck on the lips before he slipped under the covers and started snoring. And then I'd stay up another hour just cleaning and picking up and folding laundry to get ready for the next day. And on and on it went.

And I'll admit right now (it's easy because this is anonymous, haha!) that just recalling those days and the sites I looked at really tempts me to do it again. Right now…. Just read a little erotic literature and look at a few video clips. But now I know the true damage that doing so causes. So, I will be disciplined and not do it. I will wait for my husband to come home and create an even better bond with him.

Okay, so where was I… Yes, I was addicted to porn and masturbating. It's not cool, but it's the truth. It's embarrassing, but it's the truth. Sometimes I would see how many orgasms I could have in the few hours of alone time I had. What did this do for my marriage? Let's just say it wasn't good. After a few months, it was very difficult to have an orgasm during sex with my husband. And I wasn't one to fake it. He would fall asleep after and I would pleasure myself while taking a bath or right beside him while he snored.

Sometimes we would watch porn together and that would definitely help, but I felt weird having him inside me while we turned our heads to watch the television screen. It just seemed cold and like there was no real connection between us. We were making love but not looking at each other. We were making love while we were focused on something else. There was definitely a disconnect. But it kind of worked, so we kept doing it.

Eventually, it got worse and worse, and I'd rarely have an orgasm while making love to my husband. This was more than frustrating for both of us. He'd try everything to try to please me and it just wouldn't work. Where before, it was never a problem, at all.

I didn't even begin to suspect that it was my pornography and masturbating that was causing the problem. It didn't even cross my mind until I came across an article about how pornography affects the brain and can cause erectile dysfunction in men. I started researching it a bit more and decided I was going to stop. It was not as easy as I thought it would be. It took me about four months to REALLY stop. I'd try and fail, try and fail. Now it's been over 7 months since I've watched any porn or masturbated, and my marriage is on fire. When I feel the urge, I distract myself. There's always something else more productive that I can be doing. Distraction works for kids, but it also works for adults! Now, I let that pent-up arousal build and take it out on my man. (Wink, wink.) I just wait until my husband and I can get a little alone time together. And now, we make time. We go to bed at the same time (although sometimes I get up afterward and finishing cleaning the house, now) and we kiss and talk and touch each other and then make love and it's been fantastic. It took about three or four weeks, I'd say, before I started having orgasms easily again, with my husband.

I feel as though the brain is an incredible tool if you use it to your advantage. I can't wait to read your book on neuroplasticity. We have a brain so, we should get all the benefits we can from it.

Sincerely,

Sarah T.

## Testimony 3

My ex-wife and I met in college, and that's where we started viewing pornography. (In my dorm room while my roommate was at work.) Porn became a part of our life. We even subscribed to a porn site and paid $12.99 for a monthly fee for years.

We couldn't help but come across some sketchy porn movies. And some were more violent than others. I remember my wife hated these scenes and I can't blame her but they always had the opposite effect on her. They were a complete turn-off, so we tried to steer away from those.

We found ourselves eventually moving from the one-on-one sex scenes to the threesomes or group sex scenes.

These scenes were the ones we chose more often than not. We'd talk about our fantasies together and make love. As I'd make love to my wife she'd ask if I'd like to have someone join us one day. "Would you like to have another woman suck on you?" she'd ask as I made love to her. She'd continue with questions like these until I exploded, and I'll admit it was a huge turn-on.

One day, after a long day at work, I came home to find that she and her friend, Tiffany, were preparing an awesome dinner. They were giggling and drinking wine. The atmosphere was fun and relaxing. My wife told me to have a seat as she made me a drink. We drank and relaxed and laughed as our dinner was cooked in the oven.

About an hour and many drinks later, the oven timer went off and my wife pulled our meal out and set it on top of the stove. "This will need to cool before we can eat it," she said. "In the meantime I have some fruit and veggies we can nibble on." She giggled. We were all feeling a bit tipsy.

"Tiffany, why don't you sit on his lap and feed him some grapes." She handed Tiffany a small bowl of fruit. I wasn't sure I heard her correctly, but I could see the look in her eyes and couldn't believe it when Tiffany started in my direction. She was wearing a short skirt and I could tell that the alcohol was making her braver than usual.

"Your wish is my command" I remember her saying as she straddled my legs facing me. Still holding the bowl, she grabbed a large grape and slowly inserted it into my mouth. Because of the way she was sitting her skirt was practically up to her waist. As she continued to feed me, she started slowly grinding on me. As she fed me the last grape, she mashed her mouth into mine and kissed me deeply. I couldn't help but look in my wife's direction. She was looking on and came up behind me and rubbed my shoulders. "Just like in the movies, babe. Your fantasy come true. Happy early birthday."

I still couldn't believe what was happening, but it felt good. I made love to both of them and we never did end up eating dinner.

Two weekends later, Tiffany came over again. And so it continued on a regular basis. Each time we became more and more comfortable with it. The first few times it was very fast paced, sexual, and animalistic between the three of us, but as time wore on it seemed to become more sensual. Tiffany would stare into my eyes and put her hand in my hair and whisper into my ear and I started to feel an emotional connection build between us. As she'd leave afterward, I started to feel protective of her. I tell her to be safe and I meant it. I wanted her safe.

And then, my wife had to go away for the weekend, for work. As the weeks approached, and my wife talked about her upcoming trip, Tiffany and I would look at each other out of the corner of our eyes as if we could read each other's minds. We knew we were going to get together and probably my wife knew it, too. Was it cheating if my wife knew about it? Was it not cheating if my wife was there, but cheating if she was not? Where do we draw the line? It had almost become like an addiction.

I dropped my wife off at the airport and headed home. Tiffany was waiting. We were alone for the first time ever. This time, because my wife wasn't there to remind me, I didn't wear a condom. We made love and being one-on-one with her was out of this world. I could focus on her alone and she on me and I had forgotten how great that was. We made love all weekend long.

My wife never asked what I did that weekend, but I sensed that she knew. And as she went to work or to the grocery store, or anywhere, Tiffany and I would continue our alone time. I hate to say it, but I loved them both.

To make a long story short, Tiffany got pregnant. My wife and I got divorced. Tiffany and I tried to make it work, but it was doomed to fail from the start. We tried and tried, but we eventually ended up driving each other crazy. We do, however, have a daughter together now. Our daughter is a blessing, for sure, but also a reminder of what we did. Although my wife wanted to fulfill a fantasy of mine, we both ultimately betrayed her.

Moral of the story, I think porn can be okay if used wisely. Some would disagree. I think watching it as often as we did made us feel that the group sex and threesomes were something to consider. Of course, pornography is not realistic at all. I've since researched how the movies are made and it's comical really.

Now that I'm older I can see how porn can be destructive. I can't help but wonder how my life would be if I hadn't succumbed to its influence. If my wife and I had had a more pure marriage we wouldn't have even considered such a thing. And... we'd probably still be married. There's something to be said about the Ten Commandments and purity. The Bible says to think about only pure and good things. I'm still learning, but I wish I had learned a lot sooner. I wish someone would have explained the benefit to me sooner. Something I am trying to teach to my daughter now. If it can save her some heartache down the road, I will be happy.

Danny R.

## Testimony 4

I am a marriage counselor, and when I found a DVD hidden, high up in my pantry behind the pancake mix, I was very curious about it. My husband and young children were at work and school, so I popped the DVD into the player and was horrified to see that it was a porn movie. Three females going at it while one guy watched and masturbated.

Now, I like to think that I'm open-minded. I've heard it all through the years from my clients, but I've always felt that pornography is one of those difficult subjects and that it has the potential to damage relationships, for sure.

I didn't really care that my husband watched it from time to time, but I didn't like the fact that he was hiding it from me. I had a lot of questions. How long had it been going on? Were there more movies hidden around the house? How often did he watch it? I climbed up onto the cabinet counter and started looking on the high shelves. Sure enough, I found two more DVDs.

Later that night, after the kids were in bed, I sat down with my husband and asked him about them. He said that a co-worker had given them to him. This co-worker was a young female, and although she wasn't married, she had told him that she and previous partners watched the movies together. He confided to her that he wouldn't dare ask me, his wife, to watch them with him. So, she told him to just enjoy them himself. He went on to say that she confided to him that she thought it was a major turn-on for couples to watch porn together and she even told him which scenes in the movies were her favorite.

Now, I'm no rocket scientist, but I could see by the grin on his blushed red face that he was having inappropriate thoughts. I mean, how could he not? And just who was this young co-worker to give my husband porn movies to watch?!

My husband said it was no big deal and that he just stuck them up high so that the kids wouldn't find them. I told him my feelings on the subject, which he already knew. I knew the damages pornography could have on people and their families.

The porn continued. I'd place the DVD's a certain place so that I could tell if he had moved them. He was watching them almost daily. I'd confront him and he'd act like it was no big deal. I was tempted often to just throw them away, but I knew he could easily get more and deep down I feared that he'd tell his co-worker about it and that she'd laugh and giggle and give him another of her favorites. I wanted him to stop watching them on his own.

I even tried to make love to him as often as I could. I thought it would hinder his viewing the movies so often, but it didn't work. He was still watching porn almost every single day.

Approximately six months later I received a phone call at work from a woman who wouldn't give me her name. She wanted me to know that my husband was having an affair with someone he worked with. She thought I should know. My jaw hit the floor. I was extremely upset and very angry.

I flew home in a rage and confronted my husband. Sure enough, he confessed that he had been sleeping with the same woman who gave him the porn movies. He said at first, they just flirted, then she gave him the movies, then he started watching them on a regular basis, then they talked in detail about their favorites sex scenes in the movie, then she started sending him nude pictures of herself, until finally they met at her place and had sex.

I tried to make my marriage work. We went to counseling. I gave my husband more than five chances. He'd say one thing and end up doing something else. He'd move out and then move back in, move out, then move back in. He would say he was done with her then I'd find messages he sent to her saying that he missed the way she smelled. She stalked both of us. He was picking me up from work one evening because we had dinner plans and she showed up, walked into my office and started screaming and yelling. She told me many hurtful and mean things that he had said to her about me.

One time, when he had moved back in, we both went to talk to her. We were going to ask her to please give us some space and to stop contacting him. As we were walking out, I looked back and said, "He's MY husband!" She ended up punching me in the side of the head. My husband had to pick me up and carry me out. On and on things like this went for over a year until finally, I couldn't take it anymore. I felt like I was on the verge of a nervous breakdown every other week. I couldn't eat or sleep. I finally told her that she could have him. She's 15 years younger than my husband and me, and I was done competing.

I'm not saying that porn caused my divorce, but it certainly didn't help it. It was a destructive path that led to the end.

Samantha W.

## Testimony 5

My husband and I have been married for 41 years! When we were first married, our physical attraction was intense. We were very sexually active. And everything was great. I'd like to say that I knew exactly when things started to deteriorate. I mean there were many things in our lives that could have distracted us from each other but looking back now I do believe it started once we purchased our laptop and cellphones. It seems to make more sense now that I know what caused the last 15 years of our disconnect. So, about 15 years ago my husband started becoming more and more distant sexually. Instead of being sexually active 4 or 5 times a week, it went to about 4 or 5 times a month. Then those times started to even decrease. I remember being devastated when I realized that we were only being active about once a month. And in those moments my husband was experiencing erectile dysfunction. He'd get frustrated and embarrassed. He'd say that it wasn't his fault and that he didn't know why it was happening. Was it a health issue? A heart issue? An emotional issue? Was he having an affair? These were just a few of the questions I drove myself crazy with for the next three years. Then... a whole year went by and I realized that we hadn't been sexually active.... And I wanted to. I felt like I was in my prime. My husband knew I wanted to, but he just had no desire whatsoever. What was I to do? I felt like there wasn't anything I could really do. I tried changing our diet so that it was healthier. I tried turning him on. I tried reading certain books on the subject. Before I knew it 3 more years had gone by.

Then, we were at a family gathering and my husband, for some reason, couldn't log into his facebook account. As he was talking and laughing with family and friends, I took his phone and thought that I might be able to help him login. As I was fiddling with his phone and the settings, I came across a few pornography sites that he had one his phone! I was horrified by some of the titles. Group sex, gay sex, teen sex, etc. One had been downloaded five years prior. I could feel my face turn flush; it felt hot as a burning fire, as I tried to hide my emotions from everyone around me. I continued to try to get him logged in, to no avail.

I set his phone down, a million questions going through my mind. Was this a problem? How did I not know about this? He was a respected man in our community and loved by all. Did I even know my husband? After 41 years of marriage, did I even know him? Why would he be looking at gay porn? And teen porn? Disgusting!

I said nothing for weeks but did a lot of research on the subject. Come to find out, pornography can be a big problem for people, and it can spiral out of control. After watching it for a while, people need more. That is why people tend to start watching other forms of pornography. It's different, therefore, it works the brain differently.

I started leaving books and brochures, on the subject, around the house. He just shrugged his shoulders and acted like he would never do anything like that. Eventually, I shined a light on the subject, told him what I saw on his phone, and gave him an ultimatum, read the material and get help or I would consider leaving. I, we, our marriage deserved more.

At first, he didn't admit it. He denied it. But as we read the material, together, and he began to realize the powerful hold pornography had on others, he began to open up. Could this really be the cause of many of our problems?

Overall these years? Something he didn't even consider? The root of many negative issues in our lives?

My husband decided that he wanted to try to kick the habit himself. He had to learn how to be accountable and I had to learn how to be forgiving. He didn't succeed for several months but with each month it got better and better and easier and easier for him. We got a calendar and every day that he was successful, in not viewing pornography, we would draw a large heart on that day. He had to learn to be extremely honest and I had to learn how not to get mad or show my disappointment on the days he "failed".

Surprisingly this experiment brought us closer together. I mean, what did I have to lose in having him be honest with me? What did I have to lose after all this time? This experience helped us grow closer and closer to one another. I'd joke that I'd give him a "movie" to watch. I'd be his "porn star". The first month, where he succeeded in not watching porn, we celebrated! He admitted that it was extremely difficult and that he was tempted to watch it several times a day. But he did it!

During this time, we kept trying to be sexually active. His "erectile dysfunction" didn't just go away. He was still embarrassed and not sure if it would ever get better. I kept encouraging him. What did we have to lose in trying? Our relationship was better than it had been in years. At least we were talking to each other. I had to remind myself not to be resentful or angry. Yes, I deserved to be, and in the beginning, you can be sure that I expressed it, but true forgiveness is letting it go. I couldn't truly forgive him and be rude and resentful at the same time, in this process. Forgiveness is not forgetting what happened, but it is like erasing the slate clean. It's a fresh start. And although hard, it's loving and patient.

After about 8 or 9 months, we started noticing a significant difference in his libido, and he was lasting longer and longer. A few more months later and it felt almost like it did in the beginning. Some people would say that's a long time, but for 20 plus years it was getting worse and worse so comparatively 10 or 11 months is nothing, and it was so worth it.

It took strength, willpower, dedication, raw honesty, and sweat, blood, and tears, if you will. And it also took a lot of brain power and mental focus. My husband had to essentially retrain his brain. It's kind of like when someone gets in an accident and has to relearn something all over again. Of course, it's not the same, but the relearning process takes a lot of time and patience.

I hope our story can help others who may be experiencing something similar. For us, pornography addiction caused years and years of dissatisfaction and disconnect. However, since we learned how to rise above it, life is incredible again. If we can do it, so can you! Take the first step and don't look back. It's so worth it.

Veronica R.

# Conclusion

*"There is no pornography without a secrecy." ~ D. H. Lawrence*

If you, or someone you know, have been negatively affected by pornography, you are not alone. Help is available. There is a solution! Life is meant to be experienced and lived passionately, and not through a screen.

An individual's mind is the nexus to an advancement in spirituality. A healthy mind helps you to reach for, and attain, a state of spiritual readiness as you enter more mature days. On the other hand, an individual's family is the anchor that stabilizes his earthly legacy. Between mind and family, a man has his life's purpose in focus. Pornography decimates both.

In summary, pornography messes with your brain. The dopamine is released because it something you've never seen before. If one sees the same video over and over, it eventually doesn't work or have the same effect. So, the porn industry comes up with more and more and worse and worse scenarios. Porn trains and rewires our brains. This makes marriages and long-term relationships seem less satisfying. However, a real man knows this and gets true satisfaction from seeing that his partner is receiving pleasure because of him.

Pornography is unique in its effect because it's a lose-lose proposition. It really should not be taken lightly. The consumer and the performer are both on the losing end of this proposition, they are both victims.

The truth about pornography is that it is not sex. Pornography is not natural. It is voyeurism run amok and the punishment is severe for the transgressor and those who love him. Pornography tears down all involved.

On its best day, pornography can ruin the private and sacred relationship of a couple. On its worst, the addiction can cause health issues and even cross over to alcohol and drug abuse or worse.

## Where to Next

Throughout the reading of this book, you've hopefully learned facts and patterns involved with pornography you weren't equipped with before. With your new knowledge, of research backed explanations and facts, you can hopefully turn the negative impacts of pornography or any other negative factor in your sex life around and create a more rewarding and fulfilling life and relationship with the methods mentioned.

I encourage you to flip through and read this book with your partner, as well, and to have an open discussion with them. Try not to be judgmental or quick to interrupt. Confront problems you both identify in your relationship and use some of the solutions offered to help tackle them together. Use this book as a stepping stone to make your relationship and your partner a priority in your life right here, right now.

***

# About Sage Wilcox

Sage Wilcox is an author and certified energy healer and teacher. Sage enjoys traveling and giving advice to clients, friends, and family on healing, love, and relationships. Sage also enjoys studying human behavior, reading, writing, being outdoors, and enhancing relationships with others. Sage enjoys growing closer to the Divine Source and has discovered, the more we learn and practice The Word, the better life becomes. Sage is a hopeless romantic and strives to help others fall madly in love with everything about their lives! There's no room for boring in Sage's life. Sage likes to spice life up in every way! In Sage's words: "We can learn so much from each other. Here's to growing and learning, one step at a time. Let's manifest well-being, love, and unity! Let's get passionate!"

Please consider leaving a book review and visit:
http://sagewilcox.wix.com/books
www.facebook.com/sagewilcoxbooks
www.findyourwaypublishing.com

Thank you!

**Would you please consider leaving reviews, online, for my books? Reviews help more than you know, and don't have to be long; a few sentences will do. Thank you very much for your time and consideration. I am sincerely grateful.**

**Wishing many blessings to you and yours,**

~ Sage

# Other books by Sage Wilcox:

**Nonfiction:**

Love Letters from Exes: *Proof That Life Goes on After a Break Up and Love Is What You Make It*

Get It Up: *101 Ways to Raise Your Vibration, Reduce Stress, Depression, & Anxiety, Increase Joy, Peace, & Happiness and Attract Abundance Automatically!*

The 2-Hour Vacation: *Let Go and Relax, Reduce Stress & Anxiety, Gain Inner Peace, and Happiness*

The Importance of Doing It: *How to Utilize Discipline to Get Out of Bed, and Make Your Dreams Come True! A Guide to Taking Action to Create Successful Habits...*

Less Is Best: *Declutter, Organize, & Simplify to Reach Minimalism; Get More Time, Money, & Energy*

You Had Me at Re: Hello: *The Ultimate Guide to Online Dating, Including Tips and Testimonies*

Neuroplasticity and the Default Mind: *How to Shape Your Plastic Brain by Forming New Connections to Automatically Get Positive Results, Success and Prosperity*

Adjust: *How to Conquer and Accept Change and Adversity Swiftly; Stop Putting off the Love, Money, Peace, Success, and Happiness You Deserve Now*

Born New: *How to See the Familiar with New Eyes, Embrace the Magic of the Present Moment, Experience Satisfaction and Joy like Never Before*

<u>Level Up</u>: *How to Man Up and Excel When Society and Role Models Have Let You Down*

**Romance:**

    Until We Fall

    Under the Covers

    Photo Finish

    U-Turn

    Love in Troubled Waters

    Solitary Heart (With Heart Series #1)

    Awakened Heart (With Heart Series #2)

    Hopeful Heart (With Heart Series #3)

# Sources/References

**Studies that were referenced:**

**Studies:**

Gallagher, 2010

Stolerman, 2010

Hald and Malamuth, 2008

Doidge, 2007

Archives of Sexual Behavior, 2011

Lambert, 2012

Bergner and Bridges, 2002

Schneider, 2000

Zillman and Bryant, 1988

Philaretou, 2005

Archives of Sexual Behavior Study, 2011

**Authors, Universities & Journals**

William Struthers, Ph.D., author of *Wired for Intimacy*

Jill Manning, Ph.D., author of *Whats the Big Deal about Pornography*

Dawn Szymanski, 2012 the journal *Sex Roles*

Destin Stewart, University of Florida, 2012

Social Science Quarterly, 2014

Sexual Addiction and Compulsivity, Schneider, 2000

Nathaniel Lambert, Sesen Negash

Spencer B. Olmstead and colleagues

Amanda Maddox and colleagues

Andrea Mariea Gwinn, Nathaniel Lambert, and others

Journal of Sex Research

National Foundation for Family Research and Education at the University of Calgary

Susan Fiske, professor of psychology at Princeton University

Archives of Sexual Behavior. Chyng Sun and academics at Virginia Commonwealth University and James Madison University

Dr. Robert Weiss of the Sexual Recovery Institute in Los Angeles.

Ray Bergner, Ph.D., a professor of psychology at Illinois State University.

Gary Gilles, a Licensed Clinical Professional Counselor in private practice for over 20 years.

The Witherspoon Institute

Social Science Quarterly, 2004

Stanford and Duquesne Universities

Andrew Gottlieb, Ph.D., The Psychology Lounge

Sources quoted by authors

Olmstead, Spenser B., Sesen N Negash, Kay Pasley, and Frank D. Fincham, "Emerging Adults' Expectations for Pornography Use in the Context of Future Committed Relationships: A Qualitative Study," Archives of Sexual Behavior (2013), 42, 625-635.

Kimmel, Michael. Guyland: The Perilous World Where Boys Become Men. New York: HarperCollins Publishers, 2008.

Maddox, Amanda, Galena K, Rhoades, and Howard J. Markman," Viewing Sexually-Explicit Materials Alone and Together: Associations with Relationship Quality," Archives of Sexual Behavior (April 2011), 40, no. 2, 441-448.

Lambert, Nathaniel M. and Sesen Negash, Tyler F. Stillman, Spencer B. Olmstead, and Frank M. Fincham, "A Love That Doesn't Last: Pornography Consumption and Weakened Commitment to One's Romantic Partner," Journal of Social and Clinical Psychology (2012), vol.31, no.4, 410-438.

Gwinn, Andrea Mariea, Nathaniel M. Lambert, Frank D. Fincham, and Jon K, Maner, "Pornography, Relationship Alternatives, and Intimate Extradyadic Behavior," Social Psychological and Personality Science, (2013), vol.4, no. 6, 699-704.

Peter and Valkenburg, "Adolescents' Exposure to Sexually Explicit Internet Material," 595-6.

Todd G. Morrison, Shannon R. Ellis, Melanie A. Morrison, Anomi Bearden, and Rebecca L. Harriman, "Exposure to Sexually Explicit Material and Variations in Body Esteem, Genital Attitudes, and

Sexual Esteem Among a Sample of Canadian Men," The Journal of Men's Studies 14 (2006): 209-22 (216-7)

Barbara A. Steffens and Robyn L. Rennie, "The Traumatic Nature of Disclosure for Wives of Sexual Addicts," Sexual Addiction & Compulsivity 13 (2006): 247-67.

Mary Anne Layden, Ph.D. (Center for Cognitive Therapy, Department of Psychiatry, University of Pennsylvania), Testimony for U.S. Senate Committee on Commerce, Science and Transportation, November 18, 2004, 2.

Weaver, "The Effects of Pornography Addiction on Families and Communities," 3.

Michael L. Bourke and Andres E. Hernandez, "The 'Butner Study' Redux: A Report of Incidence of Hands-on Child Victimization by Child Pornography Offenders," Journal of Family Violence 24 (2009): 183-91 (187).

*Thanks again for reading this book. My goal is to help inform others and to make a positive difference with the information that I share. If you learned something beneficial from this book, please consider leaving a review online. Reviews help so much. Thank you so much for your consideration.*

# Disclaimer

The purpose of this book is for entertainment purposes only. This book is designed to provide information and motivation to our readers. The content is the sole expression and opinion of its author, and not necessarily that of the publisher. The testimonies contained in this book are from contributors and are the contributor's recollections of their experiences. This is a work based on opinions, recollections, and true events, however, names, characters, businesses, places, and incidents are either the products of the authors' imaginations or used in a fictitious manner. Any resemblance to actual persons, living or dead, businesses, companies, events, locales, or actual events is entirely coincidental. This book is not intended nor is it implied to be a substitute for professional medical advice, and any medical advice and any medical information contained in this book is not intended to be diagnostic or treatment in any way. The author and publisher are not engaged in rendering medical, psychological, legal, or any other professional services. If medical, psychological or other expert assistance is required, please talk to your physician and locate the services of a competent professional. The author and publisher shall have neither liability nor responsibility to any person or entity with respect to any loss or damage caused, or alleged to have been caused, directly or indirectly, by the information contained in this book. Neither the publisher nor the individual author(s) shall be liable for any physical, psychological, emotional, financial, or commercial damages, including, but not limited to, special, incidental, consequential or other damages. Our views and rights are the same: You are responsible for your own choices, actions, and results. If you do not wish to be bound by the above, you may return this book along with a copy of the receipt to the publisher for a full refund.

www.ingramcontent.com/pod-product-compliance
Lightning Source LLC
Chambersburg PA
CBHW030002050426
42451CB00006B/84